I0822982

EXHUMATIONS

EXHUMATIONS

JOANNE LEOW

ALCHEMY
BY KNOPF CANADA

 Published in 2026 by Alchemy by Knopf Canada, a line of books within Alfred A. Knopf Canada, a division of Penguin Random House Canada Limited, Toronto.

Alchemy by Knopf Canada, an imprint of
Penguin Random House Canada Limited
320 Front Street West, Suite 1400
Toronto, Ontario, M5V 3B6, Canada
penguinrandomhouse.ca

The authorized representative in the EU for product safety and compliance is Penguin Random House Ireland, Morrison Chambers, 32 Nassau Street, Dublin D02 YH68, Ireland, https://eu-contact.penguin.ie

A version of the chapters "Oil," "Scar," "Jewel," "Screen," and "Flight" appear respectively in *Brick: A Literary Journal*, issues 107 (Summer 2021) and 104 (Autumn/Winter 2019), *The Town Crier* (2019), *Evergreen Review* (Spring/Summer 2020), and *Release Any Words Stuck Inside of You: An untethered Collection of Shorts* (Applebeard Editions, 2018).

Library and Archives Canada Cataloguing in Publication

Title: Exhumations / Joanne Leow.
Names: Leow, Joanne, author.
Identifiers: Canadiana (print) 2025020813X | Canadiana (ebook) 20250208148 | ISBN 9781039057272 (hardcover) | ISBN 9781039057289 (EPUB)
Subjects: LCSH: Singapore—Politics and government—1990- | LCSH: Singapore—History.
Classification: LCC DS610.7 .L46 2026 | DDC 959.5705—dc23

Text and cover design: Talia Abramson
Image credit: dear sons and daughters of hungry ghosts - ila; (oil spill) sakhorn38 / Adobe Stock
Typeset by: Daniella Zanchetta

Printed in Canada

10 9 8 7 6 5 4 3 2 1

ALCHEMY
BY KNOPF CANADA
Penguin Random House Canada

For my parents and those who came before them,
known and unknown.

I never felt like I belonged where I was born, where I found myself. I felt it was necessary to reinvent myself.

Was it the blood memory of migration? The certain impossibility of return? Was it because the language in which I was most at ease, the religion in which I was carefully constrained, were only one or two generations removed? Was it the unconscious knowledge of the structures of power that unfolded like a hostile architecture around me?

Much later in life, I fell into a friendship with a writer I greatly admired. She had done a brief residency in the country of my birth. We sat across from each other in a coffee shop in my new country. When we started talking about her year in Singapore, she said to me,

"I couldn't write, I had to leave to write. I can't describe what it was. This feeling . . ."

Her voice trailed off.

Something unspoken, an understanding, passed between us then. And I knew that, somehow, she knew me and saw me. That she had started to articulate what I couldn't say. Had felt it in her bones, impinging on her flesh, her writing.

And still, it could not be set down into words. This pressure. The weight of bodies, the ever-shifting land, the detritus that covers all that we do not wish to know.

Jewel

It is my first time on a direct flight from North America to Singapore. I stumble off the plane after seventeen hours to an equatorial dawn, tempered by the brightly lit shops, air-conditioned and manicured flora of Changi Airport. The lines for those with foreign passports are long. My entrance to the country is automated, through a two-stage plastic gantry that instructs me to place my bright-red passport and then my thumb onto the appropriate glass sensors. The machine pauses, then its screen lights up, my names pressed up against each other, English and then Chinese, my selves packed into a microchip and a fingerprint record.

The signs for the new Jewel Changi, a $1.7 billion mall development at the airport, beckon as I exit the luggage claim area. I hesitate. Who does not want to see the fancy new glass-domed structure? Its centre open to the sky to accommodate the world's largest indoor waterfall. Its plants imported from all over the world, particularly the hundred-year-old trees uprooted from Spain and artfully placed amidst the luxury shops and Shake Shack outpost. The HSBC Rain Vortex, the Shiseido Forest Valley. The Manulife Sky Nets, Hedge Maze, Mirror Maze, and Discovery Slides. Even before returning to Singapore, I have seen this space from a panoply of angles, photographs of people taking selfies in front of the immense rush of water.

I demur.

Instead, I turn to the non-existent queue for taxis, ever efficiently planned for more and more visitors, and hand my bags over to the genial cab driver who greets me. As we exit the car park, he begins extolling the virtues of the Jewel and I let him go at it for a few minutes before interrupting him, my voice and accent slipping so easily into the singsong cadences of Singaporean English:

"Eh! *Macam* Singapore tourism board advertisement. Not bad yah!"

At my sly jibe, the man erupts into a high-pitched guffaw. He could not place me before, but now he has. He relaxes a little and we start to carefully negotiate conversation topics: the weather, the government, the new law clamping down on "fake news" that many of us see as an attack on freedom of speech, the prime minister's public tiff with his siblings, the endlessly changing cityscape. Life, here.

As he drives me from the eastern part of Singapore, where the airport is, we remark on the numerous trees and flower bushes that have been planted on either side of the expressway, and in the middle dividers I make out new blooms that I have not seen before.

"Those are new, right? The light-purple-pink ones?"

"Yah, always planting new things."

The topic invariably turns to the founding prime minister: Lee Kuan Yew, the driver reminds me, is the one responsible for "greening" Singapore. I return to my joking repartee with him.

"Yah lor, he planted every single tree, right?"

Another dashboard-slamming burst of laughter greets this statement. And I tell him the anecdote of the late man who, during a tree-planting ceremony, suddenly bent down to touch the pavement around a new sapling, declaring the ambient temperature a bit too warm to support its growth. We marvel at the story of his micromanagement skills, his attention to detail. I tell him about the logical offshoot of this: the National Parks trees website where, in classic Singaporean bureaucratic style, each tree is plotted out on an island map that is interactive. Click on a small green dot and you will get information on its taxonomic classification, its common name, its estimated age, and exactly how much carbon it is sequestering for our great island state.

As we continue on our journey, the driver turns my attention to the trees again. "Some of these trees too old already now, look at them, all *botak*. Dunno why. Must be the climate, or the pollution."

Samanea saman (small leaves), or rain tree. These are twenty-two years old, the map tells me later. I would have been seventeen when they were first planted.

Their branches sinuously curve in unpredictable ways before reaching canopies of delicate small leaves, softening the heat of the asphalt. They line this part of the journey from the airport to the city, strategically planted to make a good first impression on visitors to the island. Our Garden City, our Tropical City of Excellence, our City in a Garden, terraformed inside and out, already filled with trees from somewhere else. Etymologically, as the National Parks website handily informs us, *saman* is

> derived from linguistic corruption of the trees' vernacular Spanish name in northern Venezuela. Its common name, "rain tree," alludes to the tree's habit of folding up its leaves before rain, or to the shower of secretions from sap-sucking cicadas resting on it. It is hardy, tolerant of poor acidic soils and water-logged conditions.

The powers that be also know why it is dying: attacked by a fungal complex that is promoted by drought stress. A pragmatic workhorse of a tree, now suffering from the heat like the rest of us—many of its branches bereft of leaves, its bark covered in excessive lichen. I wonder what will survive in these times, in this climate, in this atmosphere, on this island of constant change, constant progress. Will we retreat to our enclosed domes, our man-made water features, the sound of water hiding the constant drone of recycled air?

I watch as the trees give way to newer specimens undoubtedly chosen for the same reasons these saplings were brought in from so far away, almost a quarter of a century ago. I watch the rows and rows of slab-like public housing mingled with tall, slim condominium apartments, new flyovers and road realignments and widenings, the clay red of soil that has been upturned for construction. When I arrive where my parents live, a set of three older, slightly mossy blocks set on the edge of a water catchment forest reserve, the driver and I conclude our conversation with the usual niceties. As I exit his vehicle, I ask for his name, shake his hand. He says this is the best conversation he has had with a customer in a long time and wishes me well before slipping back into his polished white car.

No one is there to greet me at the bottom of the slope that leads to my parents' apartment block. The humid morning air here is so different from the temperate air in the vehicle and airport I have just come from. I struggle a little, pulling my suitcases up the incline. I press the button for the elevator and watch it light up, the doors opening with a sound I have known for a very long time. I am apprehensive, afraid of seeing my mother's face, even as I cannot wait to. It is impossible to disentangle her failing body and the ever-changing island.

When I finally reach the door of the flat, I pause. I fish out the house key that I have carried across the ocean. I slip it into the lock.

Ship

After my grandmother passes, I find box after box of tiny photographs: black-and-white portraits of relatives and landscapes fixed in the sepia tones of their youth. One of them stands out. It's a rare image that shows my grandmother and grandfather with their backs towards the camera. He has his arm clasped firmly around her as they look out onto a junk boat in the distance. She has her purse clutched firmly under her right arm. It is the only time I have seen them touch.

I take a photograph of the photograph. I press my finger against the greyness of the sea. I try to imagine what they see. The old ship out to trade, the white godowns in the distance, filled with what was deemed important to the lifeblood of the Empire.

I ask my mother whether this was a photograph that she took. I notice the lower angle framing that can only come from a child holding the camera tilted slightly higher than her line of sight. In her now-halting voice, she says yes.

Oil

My grandfather started working as a mechanic for Shell after the Second World War. Following his death in 1989, my grandmother continued to receive a pension from the company. These graphite-blue slips in their envelopes came regularly for a long number of years. My grandparents' time in Borneo, that elegant terrace house in Penang, the money for my mother's convent boarding school education—all must have flowed from this oil. Yet my grandfather never told me stories about the machinery he tended to, his hand in this lucrative alchemy. He might have wondered what use a child like me would have for this knowledge. He read the newspapers to me instead, in his oddly formal English. His elocution still resonates in my head and affects my accent, my words.

My own fate finds me as a scholar of literary and cultural studies, far from my home, as an uninvited guest on Indigenous lands. When I landed my first permanent position on Treaty 6 territory and the homeland of the Métis, I knew that the salary I drew, and the federal research grants I received, arose in no small part from the wages of fossil fuel extraction and processing. Saskatchewan was where settler colonialism was extracting as much oil, uranium, and potash as it could from the prairies and boreal forests. I felt the varying rage and relief in the people around me as it became clear that the Keystone XL pipeline would never come to fruition.

I heard repeatedly about my students' families and friends whose lives were inextricably bound to the toxicities of the tar sands, the isolation of the potash mines. They worked for days on end in faraway sites, without a break, returning home to a different life in the city or a small town. What did they bring back with them, what dust, what chemicals lodged in their bodies?

Now I find myself on the unceded territories of the *xʷməθkʷəy̓əm* (Musqueam), *Sḵwx̱wú7mesh* (Squamish), and *səlilwətaɬ* (Tsleil-Waututh) peoples, working on a mountain whose side is the site of Kinder Morgan's oil storage tanks. I discover that the plan is to move 890,000 barrels of petroleum products a day right under my university's campus grounds and through the ecologically sensitive inlets and waters that surround it. Each time I take the bus up Burnaby Mountain, I glimpse the storage tanks through the windows and temperate forest, each large cylindrical structure dwarfing the humans who work there.

Reading about Canada's extractive industries, I learn that even as Shell is halving its refinery capacity in Singapore, a small portion of the oil it continues to process comes from Alberta. The provincial government's handy two-page document on the city-state reads like a cheat sheet, something that would be tucked into a carefully curated folder by the staff of Alberta Economic Development and Trade, designed to inform those who are ignorant of my island's existence. It has all the basics: capital, currency, population, GDP, key industry sectors. The cheery section entitled "Do you know?" suggests throwaway trivia of the kind one finds in a children's guide. These bite-sized facts elide the brute reality of what it means to see Singapore as "a regional hub" to "access Singapore and other priority markets in Southeast Asia and Oceania." I imagine what Albertan investors and modern-day prospectors might make of my island. Perhaps it would be familiar to them—another colonial outpost, open for business.

With the discovery of where the oil flows, it becomes a little more possible to trace the usually obscured networks of energy and extraction that extend from Indigenous lands in North America to Malaysia and Singapore, the latter's offshore islands similarly seized, terraformed.

—

"Singapore is the Houston or Rotterdam of the East," opines Bert Lotgering, the director of supplies and trading for Shell Eastern Petroleum, from his office in Shell Tower in a 1990 interview with *Forbes*. The article adopts a breathless, celebratory tone, scarcely containing its astonishment that Singapore is the "nerve centre of the Asia-Pacific region's oil economy and a chief beneficiary of its burgeoning thirst for oil." Its port is "jammed with leviathan oil tankers disgorging their cargoes of crude oil," and the country's five refineries (Shell, Exxon, Mobil, BP, and Caltex/Singapore Petroleum Company) have a capacity of about 1 million barrels per day. At its peak, this rose to 1.5 million barrels per day. The article also notes that Singapore is the oil trading centre of Asia. In 1989, the Singapore International Monetary Exchange launched Asia's first oil futures market. The government cut the income tax rate for oil traders by more than half and gave incentives for storage firms to set up tank farms.

The enthusiastic rush, the flood of figures, facts, and statistics in the *Forbes* article, lays bare the fact that Singapore has successfully positioned itself as the key node in Southeast Asia's "extractive zones." Writing from the contexts of Latin America, Macarena Gómez-Barris has defined extractive zones as ones dominated by "the colonial paradigm, worldview, and technologies that mark out regions of 'high biodiversity' to reduce life to capitalist resource conversion." Growing up, I was surrounded by such zones even as I misapprehended the orderly rows of rubber and palm trees on family drives through Malaysia. The lands and waterways around me had been transformed by centuries of treating jungles, mud flats, river estuaries, and hills as only palm oil, rubber, sand, tin, and petroleum.

Singapore does not fit the classic definition of a petro-state; it does not actually have any oil resources itself and has a diversified economy. But the republic, with its authoritarian tendencies, has since colonial times been inextricably enmeshed in the networks and infrastructures of energy production. Shell began storing kerosene on the offshore island of Pulau Bukom in 1891 and then used it as a base for the storage, blending, and reshipment of oil. Post-independence, few national narratives give enough credit to the role of oil, even as it eased Singapore's post-colonial transitions. Between 1961 and 1974, as the territory lurched from a merger with Malaysia to gaining independence from the British on its own, it went from having no oil industry to being the largest refiner in Asia. The industry benefited from the Vietnam War and Gulf wars, with Singapore's refineries supplying the American side in each conflict.

Perhaps the relation between oil and blood is why so much of this history is invisible. Ng Weng Hoong notes in his book *Singapore, the Energy Economy*, "Given the refineries' contribution to the economy and subsequent impact on the nation's political stability, there is a surprising lack of details, data and analysis on the industry's formative years in Singapore." The city-state has long camouflaged its industrialized, urban skeleton with symbolic and material veils of tropical greenery. I, like many of my peers, grew up with little to no first-hand knowledge of the refineries that guaranteed my nation's prosperity. Singapore's numerous branding campaigns (Garden City and City in a Garden) have carefully crafted its image to the world. From *Crazy Rich Asians* to Gardens by the Bay, from the lush botanical settings in *Westworld* to the indoor forests in the Jewel Changi Airport, Singapore's fecundity has been used to deflect from its oil and gas industries. Refineries have been relegated to offshore islands—quasi-corporatized spaces complete with housing for their workers, including migrant workers from Thailand, India, Bangladesh, Myanmar, the Philippines, and China. These islands, Pulau Bukom and the human-made Jurong Island, form the displaced, invisible heart of the country's industrial investments.

Jurong Island was once Pulau Ayer Chawan, Pulau Ayer Merbau, Pulau Merlimau, Pulau Pesek, Pulau Pesek Kechil, Pulau Sakra, Pulau Seraya, Pulau Meskol, Pulau Mesemut Laut, Pulau Mesemut Darat, and Anak Pulau. When the islands were amalgamated through land reclamation, the former inhabitants were evicted to make room for the oil refineries, their homes destroyed twenty years ahead of schedule. Generations of close-knit communities, maritime livelihoods, and familial geographies were buried in the sediment. In this process, the island's land area increased from 991 hectares to 3,000 hectares at the cost of $7 billion. Irene Lim describes how "the island's landscape of sprawling factories, towering chimneys, massive tanks and pipe networks set in an arid, dusty atmosphere gave it a sense of being a 'frontier land.'" The island's refineries and shipyards now employ a large percentage of Singapore's 750,000 migrant workers overseen by expatriates from America, Australia, and Europe. No one else sees these spaces anymore, save for the occasional media team.

My grandfather spent a number of years in the oil fields of Miri, Sarawak. Back then, he was the mechanic who managed the fleet of vehicles that were used by the company's executives. There was dignity in this work that has disappeared in my time. When I was a little girl, my grandmother would repeat the place name *Miri* over and over again. In the melodious, multi-tonal Penang Hokkien dialect that she spoke, the two syllables elongate in a higher pitch—*mee-ee-ree-ee*. The syllables carry with them the extravagant stories of my grandparents' time in the Shell workers' quarters, where if even as much as a light bulb went out, as my grandmother told it, the company would send someone to take care of it.

Then there is another photograph of my grandparents with their backs facing the camera. My grandmother is dressed in an impossibly immaculate and elegant cheongsam, my grandfather's arm linked to hers. She is reaching out to grasp a tall Caucasian man's hand. She was so proud of this photograph. She calls him "Hông-thài-chú," the prince. Only many years later will I realize that the man in the photograph is Prince Philip, Duke of Edinburgh, during his forty-one-hour 1959 visit to Sarawak, to inspect the workings of Empire. My grandmother, even as she was unable to speak English, revelled in this memory of her brief encounter with the British monarchy, her recollection more vivid than any palm-sized photograph. Among the same set of mementoes, I find a typewritten letter, its paper yellowed with age, commending my grandfather for the efficiency and reliability of the cars used for the prince's visit—the closest the both of them had come to the heart of the Empire that required their labour and adoration.

The Upper Miocene Miri Formation deposited by the paleo-Baram delta determined the destiny of this coastal settlement. The Miri field lasted sixty-one years before it was closed, with 625 wells and a total volume of 80 million barrels of oil. The first workers in the field had come from Singapore. I try to imagine my young grandfather, his lithe frame moving in the shadow of Miri Well No. 1, the Grand Old Lady, now merely a historical monument. I know he worked for the Japanese when they took over the oil field and then for Shell when the war ended. There were no stark differences between these imperial projects—only an allegiance to keeping the oil flowing. Part of the site was christened "Canada Hill" after the Canadians who made it all the way to Miri in the middle of the twentieth century to help with the drilling. They most likely came from the town Petrolia, Ontario, where the discovery of oil fields in the 1850s dispossessed the Ojibwe, Potawatomi, and Odawa peoples. In a 1924 *Maclean's Magazine* article, Victor Lauriston calls Petrolia "the unquestioned metropolis of the pioneers of oil," borne out of "the thousands of three-pole pumping derricks that . . . dot the Lambton landscape." When that oil ran out, "oil-splattered emissaries" were sent out to ruin other lands.

Amitav Ghosh famously coined the term *petrofiction* to designate an already uncommon narrative form: novels and stories that make oil and the oil industry their main themes. Few authors seek out oil as a literary trope since, as Ghosh writes, "oil smells bad. It reeks of unavoidable overseas entanglements, a worrisome foreign dependency, economic uncertainty, risky and expensive military enterprises; of thousands of dead civilians and children and all the troublesome questions that lie buried in their graves." In his review of Abdelrahman Munif's *Cities of Salt*, Ghosh notes how "a great deal has been invested in ensuring the muteness of the Oil Encounter: on the American (or Western) side, through regimes of strict corporate secrecy; on the Arab side, by the physical and demographic separation of oil installations and their workers from the indigenous population." He argues that the "territory of oil is bafflingly multilingual" and "the experiences associated with oil are lived out within a space that is no place at all, a world that is intrinsically displaced, heterogeneous, and international." It seems fitting here to think of the offshore islands in Singapore, their communities dispossessed, their land forcibly reduced to mere economic value.

Forces of extraction transform territory and community. What do they leave us with? What cultural forms might we need to reconsider to encounter oil in Singapore? And, to elaborate on a question posed by Jennifer Wenzel, if Singapore is a success story written in no small part by petroleum, how do we read for oil? Petrofictions produced in Singapore that confront the commodity and the industry directly are as rare and elusive as Ghosh predicted. There is no long poem about refineries, no great novel about the machinations it took to launch the futures market, and certainly no mainstream publisher eager to work with the ones who toil in the dangerous mazes of stacks and pipes. The problem goes beyond a simple lack of access to the physical spaces of oil refining and extends to the state's reluctance to advertise the presence of its massive fossil fuel industry in favour of a global City in a Garden mirage.

Increasingly, I see Singapore as a petrofiction in and of itself. Its true nature erupts every now and again, in the roar of a sports car down its impossibly well-kept roads and the smell of the crude wafting across the coast.

—

The year 1961 saw both the opening of the island's first refinery and the first iteration of the Singapore Grand Prix. The annual race ran until 1973, after which it was deemed too dangerous to continue. The circuit included the tree-lined spine of an old colonial road just north of my childhood apartment. Unknowingly, I have driven down that leafy stretch of the track countless times. Black-and-white photographs from that first race show Singapore's first president, Yang di-Pertuan Negara (Lord of the State) Yusof Ishak, being driven around the course by the president of the Motor Club. He is dapper in his suit and perfectly coiffed hair. His wife, the twenty-eight-year-old Noor Aishah, is dressed in the traditional sarong kebaya as she presents the trophy to Ian Barnwell, winner of Singapore's first Grand Prix.

The Formula One consortium brought the race back in 2008. Sponsored by government-linked companies like Singtel and Singapore Airlines, the Singapore F1 night race is petrofiction at its finest. Its essential qualities of speed, technical prowess, competition, danger, and thrill embody the effects and powers of oil. It is a seductive, desirable encounter, narrated through the drama of its drivers and teams and built on the fiction of endless supply. While the refineries may be invisible to tourists and the general populace, the night race is impossible to ignore:

The central business district is shut down; hundreds of thousands of tourists descend; the high-pitched whine of the engines can be heard far into the heartlands; and what CNN calls "a bonanza of weekend entertainment, which includes everything from concerts with A-list singers to luxurious parties" ensues. The aerial views of the illuminated racetrack, with its 1,600 light projectors simulating daylight for the drivers, are the luminous arteries of oil made visible amidst downtown Singapore's mix of colonial and contemporary architecture. In 2019, 268,000 spectators showed up for the race, despite the hazardous levels of haze that filled the air due to forest fires in neighbouring Indonesia.

—

I only came to know my grandfather after he stopped working for Shell. He smoked a pipe, played cricket, and listened to the BBC World Service. His favourite dish was "chicken stew"—an English chicken soup spiked with the spices of the Malay world: whole stewed cinnamon, nutmeg, peppercorns, and star anise. His skin was dark brown after hours of outdoor sports and working. He wore thick black-rimmed glasses, combed his hair back neatly. I have a tape of him reading the newspaper, pronouncing his strict, clipped syllables. He left me a worn copy of *The Imitation of Christ*, a letter opener shaped like a kris, and a Ronson lighter engraved with his initials, made in England. I try to imagine him with the lighter, the smell of pipe smoke, and his starched shirts, hand laundered and pressed by my grandmother. He went to London once in his life, in the early 1960s. I remember his palpable shock and distaste, even after so many years. He told me with dismay that he had seen people there who were so poor all they could afford was chips wrapped in newspaper, and no fish, which was the cheapest protein source of the archipelago he had grown up on. How could this be the centre of the world?

—

Echoes of the metropole underpin the Singapore writer Clara Chow's dystopian short story "The Wheel." In the near future, Singapore is a hyper-surveilled, carceral state with its oil refineries lying in toxic, polluted ruins and its population rendered inexplicably infertile. Chow was inspired by the artist Chun Kai Feng's installation piece *Ride of a Lifetime!*, which turns the Singapore Flyer, an easily recognizable symbol of tourism (and a copy of the London Eye), into a form of maximum-security imprisonment. Chow begins her story with this premise:

> There are twenty-eight capsules, each the size of a small bus. They are glorified oil drums, rolling as the giant wheel spins—a clever engineering trick

> so that we are never upside down, nor reduced to hamsters on a treadmill.
>
> Twenty-eight people in each capsule, walls of metal separating us into cells. Strapped to vertical gurneys, we sleep upright at night. The carpet has been worn bare in patches. In the day, we stand, shifting from balls to heels, heels to balls, trying not to touch anything shiny, metal encasing our meat. Burns, when we get them, take a terribly long time to heal. The smell of seared flesh shades from fried beef to charcoal.

Here, the tourist attraction, as in Chun's art piece, is reduced to its constituent, seemingly pointless parts, a giant wheel that goes nowhere, studded with "glorified oil drums"—one in a series of references to oil in the story. The wheel is in stasis even as it is continuously in motion—a metaphor for economic progress vis-à-vis the continued repression of human rights in Singapore. Motion is coupled with imprisonment, and the state's concealment of the longer histories of detention without trial is laid bare through this reverse panopticon, with the prisoners always in view.

As the first story that Chow wrote for her debut collection, "The Wheel" sometimes feels like a collision of all the contradictions, whispers, and scars of modern Singaporean history: There are arbitrary imprisonments, the torture of political dissidents, a preoccupation with women's bodies and their fertility, the literalization of a nanny state that takes in children from China as part of an economic agreement. The story starts with an unlikely prison break and the creation of a temporary utopian colony on the offshore island of Pulau Hantu, an escapade that is ultimately shown to be part of an elaborate reality show staged by the state: "*Lord of the Flies* meets *Animal Farm*, leading to a gory end. A cautionary tale against communism or any sort of revolution."

While it is possible to read the anxieties and excesses in the story in numerous ways, I am struck by the story's repeated references to the post-industrial, post-oil landscape of the offshore islands that surround its imagining of Singapore. In the story's world, there has been a catastrophic industrial accident at the "Clam Oil Refinery on Pulau Bukom" leaving its neighbouring islands with contaminated soil and water. The story hints that this may have also contributed to the sterility of the population.

As the escapees journey away from Singapore's mainland to establish a small commune, one of the characters recalls present-day Singapore, our contemporary moment:

> Decades ago, people had come to Pulau Hantu to get away from the stresses of the over-developed mainland. You boarded a ferry at Marina South Pier, letting the sea breeze cover you in mist

> until your thin clothes are soaked as the little boat wove its way like a gnat past the big Chinese tankers parked offshore, waiting to be loaded or unloaded of containers of goods. Tankers with names like 秋池 (autumn pond), 大球 (big ball), and 新发现 (new discovery). You watch the mainland coast unfurl like a fantascope: the skyscrapers giving way to millionaires' homes on Sentosa Cove, and then to the white cake-like structures of Jurong Island's energy and chemicals industry. . . .
>
> You catch a whiff of bitumen, bunker oil, kerosene and diesel in the air, as Pulau Bukom glides into sight—a sign that you're approaching Hantu.

Unlike the sleek contours of the F1 petrofiction, this detailed parsing of the seascapes and littoral zones of southern Singapore allows us to observe and experience their incongruous layers. Transnational circuits of crude in Chinese tankers. Exclusive housing built undoubtedly in part from the profits from extraction, the refining and trading of fossil fuels. The refineries themselves are, in this instance, juxtaposed as closely as they are linked in real life. Even though it is offshore, out of sight most of the time, what gives the petroleum away is the olfactory—the "whiff of bitumen, bunker oil, kerosene and diesel" in the air, in the atmosphere, invisible but present. When the escapees are recaptured by the state and placed back into their rotating jail, the story describes the gruesome spectres that haunt one of its main characters, Mae: those who have been hanged by the state, those who were collateral damage in their escape.

It's curious, however, that these offshore islands are also haunted by another set of ghosts: those involved in the failed bombing of the Pulau Bukom Shell refinery in 1974, touted as Singapore's first brush with international terrorism. Two members of the Japanese Red Army and two members of the Popular Front for the Liberation of Palestine attempted to blow up the refinery. They wanted to strike a blow against Western imperialism and disrupt the oil supply from Singapore to South Vietnam in solidarity with the revolutionary forces. During their attempt, they deceived and enlisted the help of a Malay fisherman. Chow's story confabulates the interactions between the would-be bombers and the fisherman. Making small talk, the fisherman tells them of the "Garoupa, ikan batang, ikan bawal hitam, toman . . . udang" that fill these waters. They bond briefly over this knowledge, suggesting other, anti-colonial ways of reading this historical episode, other ways of seeing these coastal waters, the suppressed histories of Singapore's oil, and the wars it was used to fight:

> *I think of the Malay fisherman and his scowling, skittish passengers now, as I see the lights of a fishing*

boat, like phosphorous barnacles, gliding towards the opposite shore.

They are here. More ghosts.

Chow's dystopian Singaporean future is haunted by failed anti-imperial, anti-petroleum acts, and the detritus of its energy ambitions. Its refineries have shut down, they are "steel ruins, unspeaking remains . . . the industrial wasteland." Neglect, as the story puts it, is also a form of reclamation.

How does one escape these petrofictions? These ghosts of oil? I don't know what I am looking for, really, as I plumb the internet for the safety records of oil refineries in Singapore and beyond. I encounter nothing but corporate speak and declarations of the various companies' adherence to the Modern Slavery Act. One phrase stands out: ExxonMobil's mantra for its safety program is "Nobody gets hurt."

My grandfather never talked about his time as a mechanic for Shell or for the Japanese. He died of emphysema when I was nine—whether from his years smoking or his years working with volatile hydrocarbons in the air, we will never know.

Blood

When we are twelve, the vans arrive at the school, each with a nurse, a photographer, and two bureaucrats. They unload a series of grey folding tables from their vans, they set up microscopes, stacks of forms, pads of ink, and a white-curtained backdrop for pictures.

We are told that this is the day we will be getting our identity cards. We line up in our white-and-blue uniforms, our ponytails at regulation length, our shoes whitewashed and laced, our socks no higher than our ankles. When I get to the front of the line, I am told to hold out my left index finger and the nurse places it in between the jaws of what looks like an oversized stainless steel stapler. Before any of us can protest, she clamps the stapler down and instantly a large drop of blood appears on the tip of my digit. Working quickly, she takes my hand and squeezes the drop out onto a glass film, dismissing me with a bit of cotton to staunch the bleeding.

We file one by one to have this done. I do not remember fear. We did not know what would be encoded into the pink plastic cards that would appear in our mailboxes in two weeks. We did not think about how we become a number. About how we would be quantified and catalogued and placed neatly into a column.

We are thumbprinted, photographed, and dispatched. We are assigned numbers beginning and ending with a single letter. The same sequence of numbers for our birth certificates, our passports, our library cards, our driver's licences. Each time we register for a service, we recite this number unbidden, unconscious. It becomes an incantation, a talisman, a poem that never rhymes.

—

In just a few years, I will begin to understand what this means when I face a table of older men who will decide what will happen in the next decade of my life. As they begin to ask me questions about what I want, what my hopes are, what my gifts are, my talents, my aptitudes, I begin to realize that their decision has already been made. I have already been reduced to a series of scores and notes that are scattered over a clutch of papers photocopied into identical sets of files that sit before them.

I shift in my seat, my body unused to the business suit that I have put on for the occasion, an eighteen-year-old attempting to dress as her twenty-something future self, the vibrant yet polite hope of the nation.

—

Many years later, I take a class where I learn how to hit things without causing myself any pain. Elbows, knees, shins must make contact with another human body at precise points. My own body, with its idiosyncratic angles and geometries, is unforgiving of mistakes. It's a tender ligament, a loose tendon chastising itself. Every day brings a new disappointment, some failing, some inflexibility, some misstep that I did not notice before.

I persist, I wrap my hands tighter in preparation, bind my wrist bones and knuckles into place, hold my small fists up on either side of my face, raise my shoulders into my neck.

Sometimes, I look at each point on a face that I want to punch, each soft and hard part of that body politic, I see it in the bag in front of me. I drive first my jab, then my cross into its jaw. I learn how to swivel my hips just so, my sockets and joints open to new motions, new ranges. My kicks connect to kidney, spleen, liver, heart. The hook of my foot catches my opponent's knee as I aim to bring them closer to me.

Fix

I ask my younger son if he remembers a time when my mother was not ill, when her body was not stiffening, her neurons and synapses unable to speak to her limbs. He does not. My older son does, but just barely.

I try to jog their memories, remembering my mother's care with my first-born. The way she shooed me away for an extra nap when he fell asleep. Her visits to the local library, emerging with carefully chosen board books for the children.

I want them to remember her this way.

My father took a photograph of her and my two small boys when she was just on the brink of her illness; only the occasional loss of balance, a fall, would hint at the impending. He makes a decoupage from scratch, permanently affixing the picture to a piece of wood. Their smiles frozen, my sons always four and six. He applies an acrylic resin to the piece, hoping it will last for as long as we need it to. But he is mistaken. It is not stillness and fixity that we need. If oil and blood are both circulatory systems, if both depend on each other, then what branching paths and conduits do they take? We want to freeze moments in time: pixel to ink to emulsion, each substance sustainable only by the by-products of extraction. Our memories forever fixed in some form of plastic.

Do the last days of my mother's life need such fixity? None of the intricate currents throughout her body seem to be functioning as they should. Blockages, mis-recognitions, miscommunications, misfirings.

Her heart will fail from these exertions, halt her pulse. An empty well.

Flight

My older son, aged five or six, riding in the alleyway behind our first apartment in Toronto. His new bike, the Norco Mity Macho, red and shiny in the late summer afternoon.

We're standing a ways from him, talking of trivialities, when in the corner of my eye I see him round a corner and flip down to the ground. He screams.

The twenty or so metres between him and us seems interminable as we run to the end of the alleyway. He is distraught, his chest covered in blood from what we later realize is simply a gash on his chin.

At that moment I can only think of major arteries and veins.

He leaves his bicycle, a small pool of blood, and we do the usual: a hasty car ride, emergency room, fixing up. He gets a tetanus shot that was overdue.

—

I have been thinking recently about flight, departures, distance, and return. Forced return, emergency return, unknown return. The untraversable distance between parent and child.

When did these thwarted departures begin?

My mother turning from me when I first got my acceptance to a liberal arts college in the improbable state of Rhode Island. Speaking through the grilles of our front gate,

"You'll never come home again."

A throwaway line that I repeat to friends as an explanation of our relationship.

She lined that first suitcase with gifts, sweetmeats, biscuits, new clothing, old clothing, fears. The latter proved to be founded. An affair, unknown to them, with its secret goodbyes in the anonymous stairwells of the airport. An errant electronic missive minutes later finding its mark in the wrong inbox.

Flight.

—

My last real departure was unattended.

When we arrived at the departures terminal, my father left his keys in his locked car with the engine running. A family friend drove him back to our home to retrieve a spare set. For forty minutes, the car was left parked illegally outside the terminal, its hazard lights flashing, its machinery emitting a soft, uneasy purr.

My mother refused to wait with me. Refused to stay either inside or outside the terminal. We began an awkward pas de deux, with family friends offering to watch the car while we spent time either in the cold, impossibly high-ceilinged terminal or outside, in the deepening evening heat.

Or even at that threshold, where the temperate flow of conditioned air meets with the humidity. The opposite of a gap. Too much air, each of a different density and temperature, each unyielding, an invisible border that you cross even before you leave.

I had packed my own suitcases.

—

I see my parents together in Canada a few more times. Always at airports now. We say goodbye out of habit. We say hello as if it is a forgotten word.

They call me "girl." As if there isn't another.

The last time, I wait longer than the stipulated time in the arrivals terminal at Pearson. They are disgorged by the sliding doors, in a windbreaker and a cardigan. And I want to tell them that here there is no difference between the air inside and out. Not such a big difference, in any case. But I don't.

We leave to return to depart again. When we are in the cab on the way to Toronto, my mother speaks in the old dialect,

"Even if you paid me, I wouldn't move here."

—

In the emergency room, a man recognizes me from another life.

"Are you? Did you?"

"Yes."

"Funny, I thought so."

I smile at him, holding my son's hand. Resident, exile, expatriate, immigrant, the distance between those words not far as they stitch my son's chin together with a glue that was invented for war wounds.

In a week, he will be back on his bicycle. In a few years, he will be pedalling beside me, keeping pace on the sidewalk as I negotiate between truck and parked car.

An object in flight.

Face

"I'm going to do half your face and you're going to do the other half."

I look at the makeup artist with some confusion. I have just started my job reading the daily bulletins for the only news channel in Singapore. He is responsible for ensuring that I look as flawless and convincing as possible when I recite the headlines of the day. He patiently repeats himself,

"I'm going to do half your face and you're going to do the other half."

He begins to draw an invisible line down the middle of my face with his foundation sponge. As I watch in the mirror, the left side of my face becomes an accentuated version of itself. My brow darkens; my cheekbone elevates; my eye is outlined; and half my lips are reddened. He takes out a silver eyelash curler from his case and asks me to lower my eyelids as he carefully inserts my lashes into the contraption. He avoids the paper-thin skin attached to the hairs there. Before I can protest, he closes the jaws of the crimp. He removes the device and I open my eyes. I look wide-eyed and doe-like on one side.

"All right, now it's your turn."

Under the watchful eye of the makeup artist, I begin the other half of my face. I erase every blemish, every freckle and wrinkle, from my skin. I fill in the fine lines under my eyes, the skin there ever so slightly darker than the rest of my face. The foundation marks as it erases. Later, I will call it battle paint. I pick up another brush and spread a light-pink hue on my eyelid, repeating the gesture with grey and then another brush with dark eyeliner. I use yet another brush on my cheekbone, endowing it with a faint blush. A dewy-eyed bride I am.

We look at my face in the mirror. The makeup artist frowns. He points out my faulty lines, my clumsy attempts at shading, how all my angles are wrong. My face, before us, is asymmetrical. I wonder what else might be wrong, under my skin, in my bones, in my cells.

He soaks a cotton pad in an expensive Japanese cleansing oil and starts to smear off all the colours on my face. It smells floral, yet its unctuous texture gives it away all the same.

"Let's try this again."

Rights

An assembly which was not unlawful when it assembled may subsequently become an unlawful assembly.

—SINGAPORE PENAL CODE, CHAPTER VIII, SECTION 141

It is the unspoken legislation that permeates all public spaces in the country. There can be no assemblies without a permit from the police. An assembly is so broadly defined, it can now even mean just one person. When I am a little girl, I am conditioned to cringe at hoarse opposition politicians shouting their causes at the entrances of subway stations and shopping centres. Their voices amplified by the concrete structures all around them. I turn away, I walk faster.

But there are always assemblies as I am growing up. Assemblies that begin when I am two or three, where I mouth the words to an anthem in a language that does and does not belong to me. There we stand in impeccably straight lines, pressed uniforms, pinned badges. Echoes of Empire, God, Queen, President, and Republic dictating each movement. Hands at our sides, hands behind our backs, right fists to our hearts. These are assemblies, but we are not assembling.

There are religious meetings with folk guitars, competitions for sanctity, for proximity to Church, priest, youth leader. Later, this is not something I want at all.

When I leave the country, it always surprises me when my new acquaintances assemble so easily—for causes that I sometimes did not even know existed. I go once, when it seems necessary to avert a war, an unjust invasion, an occupation. When the burden of truth against so much falsehood seems too much to bear and must be experienced collectively. There are rainbow-coloured flags with the Italian word for peace on them. *Pace*, they say, asking us to pace ourselves. Later, there are megaphones, poetry readings, mocking speeches, dominant personalities. I am not sure that these are assemblies as much as assemblages, each part moving independently, seeking attention, affecting the whole.

So, I am wary of walking in a line, of chanting, of repetition, of zeal. I am wary of repeating what one person has said without turning the words over in my mouth first, like a series of small rocks that need to be smoothed into pebbles that spill out to be stepped on. I wince at photographs of myself taking on causes—even ones that I believe in.

This is what growing up in a place without assemblies does to you. How can one combination of bodies in one space be lawful and another set of bodies in another place unlawful? What does resistance mean? At what point do bodies, walking in circles, hands aloft, drunk on music and chants, cross a line that divides the affective and the absurd? What does it mean to be skeptical in the face of zeal? To resist having your body and the bodies of your children put in a line for any particular cause?

In graduate school in Toronto, there is always a sneaking suspicion in my peers that my success came from some kind of compromise. Perhaps it did. But how else to survive that dislocation, how else to escape? What they see as some kind of stylish guile, that confident voice born out of years of training and discipline, those old blazers from work—these were all hard-earned tokens from a bond, a life without choices. One of my peers delights in her cruel way of pointing out that I do not "understand how power works," that my politics are impure, my allegiances suspect, my ambition unseemly. She will walk past me in the corridors of the department, face turned to the wall. She will refuse to acknowledge the fact of my existence.

I will never understand this hatred, this wish for my erasure. Was it ignorance? Racism? An inability to see me like everyone else is: as a constellation of intersecting and complicated forces? I have such a different comprehension of power from her. But I lack the vocabulary to explain myself. My body is disappeared, invisible in her calculus.

Still

There is not a single human figure in the photographer Darren Soh's coffee-table book *In the Still of the Night (While You Were Sleeping).* His uncanny images were photographed in total darkness with shutter speeds of up to five minutes. Of his work in this book he notes, "I wanted to bring to my audience's attention a side of Singapore that most would not see, and even if they saw, would not notice."

The long shutter speeds give the photographs an otherworldly hue, heightening the scope of our limited sight. Their slower, contemplative methods bleed into their subjects. A photograph of migrant workers' dormitories in 2014 depicts them looking nearly idyllic next to Sungei Punggol, a small river in the northern part of the country. The squat, identical buildings have external balconies and staircases decorated in rainbow hues, exoskeletons that are red, orange, yellow, green, and blue. The gradient of the sky is lavender and mauve. These buildings, the S11 dormitories, will be the epicentre of the COVID pandemic in Singapore. The workers' living conditions, four square metres a person, practically guarantee their infection.

Most of us never see the dormitories for what they are unless it is to criticize their proximity to housing for Singaporeans. That is the only time their presence perforates our everyday reality. Then the workers become a threat to the neighbourhoods, schools, public housing blocks, streets, and parks next to which they happen to be living. Never mind the fact that they and their predecessors were the ones who built these planned landscapes, following the orders of the authorities, the architects, the planners, their supervisors. They laid the rebar, poured the concrete, painted the walls, and continue to clear the rubbish chutes, and painstakingly weed and prune back any errant shrubbery. The very spaces where they are seen as unwelcome intruders. There are a million and a half of them now, their numbers increasing with the exponential growth of Singapore's economy at the start of the new millennium.

How do we house that many workers? I study the website for ASPRI, a company running worker dormitories. Their publicity matter features photographs of the workers, smiling at the camera from their narrow galley kitchen, demonstrating how they might cook their meals. The floor plan of each unit is efficient, eight bunk beds pushed together as close as they can possibly be. What is most important, as the company notes, is exactly how close the workers are to their work sites. After all, they are useless unless they are labouring. They are transported in the flimsy backs of small pickup trucks that have no seat belts, since they were only intended to convey construction materials. Every year there are horrific, often fatal accidents.

—

In other photographs by Soh, we see the evidence of migrant labour in the portraits of building cranes, the muddy tracks of their wheels, excavators slumped as if in prayer, dams, sand piles, trucks without drivers that are filled with gravel or mutilated trees. Soh's images pull off the cover of darkness that prevents us from perceiving the pace of change, the workers themselves invisible spectres hovering just beyond the frame. Can one hold the din and the violence of the labour that must happen for this "development," even as we admire the sculptural form of a Kobelco at rest? This is the forgetting that it takes to sustain the island's perfection. Soh's photographs, haunting and technically proficient as they are, make it easier for us to look the other way.

In Singapore, migrant workers, whether employed in construction work or the never-ending tasks of domestic drudgery, elder care, and child care, are unable to achieve any other status in the country. They cannot marry a Singaporean, the women are deported if they opt to carry a pregnancy to term, they are subjected to intrusive medical examinations every year, and they are not afforded the protections of labour laws. The scholar Charan Bal uses the term "deportability" to describe the status of these workers in Singapore. He argues that it is their "deportable legal status . . . that renders their labour power a 'distinctly disposable commodity.'" The workers are seen as "disposable economic subjects" rather than persons with rights, values, and choices.

What does it mean not to be a person but just a part of an efficiently run machine? On one of the rare occasions migrant workers rioted in Singapore, the state blamed the disorder on public drunkenness, but perhaps it came from a realization of how little their lives meant to those exploiting them. Maybe the alcohol was a salve, a balm, a way to cope with the relentless shifts, the ingratitude of those who profited off their labour, and their longing for home. The catalyst for the unrest was the sight of one of their own, dead and pinned under a bus that had refused to drive him back to his dormitory. The official report would later fault Sakthivel Kumaravelu for his own death.

Diagnosis

My father says he started to notice it when she was unable to fill in forms. Her usual angular handwriting turning into illegible scribbles. She became depressed, unlike herself. She lost so much weight at one point that everyone, herself included, believed she had some form of cancer.

Then there is one terrible fall that sends her to the hospital. An astute neurologist putting the pieces together and attempting some form of diagnosis.

When I am away, my father sends me pictures of my mother—in the park, at the table, smiling with friends as if there is nothing wrong. When she first falls down, he sends me a picture of her face, bloodied; her eye, swollen.

—

I try to make sense of this long trajectory of decline. I watch my mother on the screen. Sometimes it takes me a while to realize the video isn't frozen. The quality occasionally turns sharp, sharper than I can bear. I have a pocket-sized window into my childhood home. The distinctive two-note call of a koel sometimes audible through my speakers. My mother's face is often immobile, unable to smile, her hand fixed into a wizened fist. Increasingly, her mouth stays open like a baby bird's, and her expression is one of permanent wonderment at the world moving on around her.

My father sends me an MRI image. It is a side profile of her head, her brain stem atrophying. I keep this on my phone even as it is unbearable to look at.

> Progressive supranuclear palsy is characterized by decreased cognition, abnormal eye movements (supranuclear vertical gaze palsy), postural instability and falls, as well as parkinsonian features and speech disturbances.

This is what it is like to recognize your mother in a medical textbook. This is what it is like to be unable to read her writing and her brain scan.

I parse the instructions from the online guide for radiologists in training: radiopaedia.org. How does one read these images? I try for the vocabulary of it all. There are all these words I have rarely encountered for parts of the brain I didn't even know existed: anteroposterior midline midbrain, superior colliculi, interpeduncular fossa, intercollicular groove, tegmentum. Parts, locations, an indented line to run my finger across.

I notice how these words don't seem enough for the specialists; the guide speaks of hummingbirds, penguins, and morning glories. These are signs taken for tragedies. I imagine the wing flaps of birds flying and swimming in my mother's skull. Loss of the lateral convex margin of the tegmentum of midbrain. Her errant brain blossoming in flowers that last only a day.

—

> Your brainstem is responsible for a large number of vital functions, including your ability to swallow and hold your body steady (your posture). Your basal ganglia also help with posture, as well as eye movements, thinking and emotions.

What random genetic mutations (the indecipherable row after row of letters and numbers, of sequences)?

Which unknown infectious agents?

In the air, water, or food?

What unknowable chemical? How slow was this damage, this violence?

Was it the traffic, the atmosphere, the invisible plumes?

Was it transferred by clothing, upholstery, carpet, plastic file holders? How long ago did it start?

How might any of us stay uncontaminated by all that was built around us?

Sand

In the year after I leave Singapore for graduate school in Toronto, the stunning eco-development Gardens by the Bay opens to the public. Built on land reclaimed from the sea, the one-billion-dollar project has the singular goal of being spectacular. It is, of course, an unbridled success. After all, in this country, this has been planned for years in advance: Sand, earth, and soil were taken from hills in the island's interior starting in the 1970s to increase the country's size by 350 hectares. Then, when that ran out, it was dredged from islands belonging to Malaysia and Indonesia, and from river estuaries in Vietnam and Cambodia. This is new land, an Eden that sits and stabilizes before it is ready as tabula rasa.

First, they hold an international design competition to attract the world's best architectural and landscaping firms. The famous Israeli-Canadian architect Moshe Safdie successfully pitches an "integrated resort," adding to his already prolific portfolio of monumental developments in

Singapore. The British firm Grant Associates is selected to be the lead designer for the Gardens by the Bay project. In a slew of promotional videos that seek to depict their vision for the site, they declare, "On a plate, this is what Singapore is about." A breathless proclamation that is set to vaguely Oriental music with animated red lanterns bobbing in the background. In a few years, the internet and social media feeds will be awash with footage of the Marina Bay Sands, its casino and rooftop pool, and the Gardens seen from every possible vantage point—lush, tropical, manicured, and futuristic all at once.

I become obsessed with these ostentatious spaces, seeing the Supertrees as concrete monstrosities, covered with creeping epiphytes and lit up with neon and lasers for a nightly show. I study the construction photographs, the red earth upturned and the naked concrete pylons that form the skeleton of the garden. I can barely explain my rage at the cooled conservatories built by migrant workers who have been labouring at breakneck speed to cut costs and finish the project before its over-bloated budget gives way. I find it difficult to explain to others why I am moved to so much anger by this carefully engineered feat of horticultural excellence—an ambitious confluence of architecture and landscaping on prime downtown land. I know how I must sound: odd, dissonant, out of pace, out of breath.

I visit the space a few times with trepidation. I take note of all the signs that forbid so many things but especially the touching of plants. There is signage that bids me to take fixed routes through the Cloud Forest, a concrete building within a glass dome that has been completely draped with montane vegetation. I learn that there are 225,000 plant species here, including a thousand-year-old olive tree from Spain that was imported here. The tree was slated for destruction in any case, they say, and so the horticulturalists have saved it from its inevitable fate. Parts of the temperate world have found their way into this meticulous showground and its twin, the Flower Dome—replications and reversals of the structures of power that made Kew Gardens in London the metropole of colonized flora.

The domes are maintained at a pleasant temperature. Quietly, workers toil in the background in a constant battle with dead foliage and other challenges. There are no insects or birds. An energy consumption study finds that there is no difference between the conservatories and an average commercial building. I watch as the tourists and Singaporeans take selfies amidst an enormous tulip display, bulbs imported from Europe, bursting into Technicolor blooms here on the equator.

But it's the sand that starts to nag at me. The sand needed to create this new land, arriving at the ports on open barges in ever-larger quantities. The architect and geographer Joshua Comaroff calls it "an unstable and promiscuous alternative, quickly drained of historical and geographical traces . . . [it] holds allegiances to no nation, no religion. Its form is transience." Comaroff notes that it is not just horizontal expansion that Singapore needs sand for, but vertical growth as well—fine river sand for beaches and concrete, coarse sea sand for new ground. He points out that "sand, like money, must remain liquid for the economy to keep moving." All I can think is that, when it is transmuted into land and buildings, is it not occupation in a different form? Have we not seized someone else's land for our profit, for our entertainment?

—

I become acquainted with the work of the Singapore conceptual artist Charles Lim. He has spent two decades compiling the material evidence of the state's slow but colossal alterations of its shorelines. It is an idiosyncratic and often surreal documentation, but one that persists in bearing silent witness to the loss of Singapore's indigenous coastal flora and geography, and the concurrent construction of massive infrastructural projects on its "new lands." I sit with his work *SEA STATE*, all its iterations, from photography, digital images, remedial cartographies, intertidal garden installations, and experimental films to a haunting twenty-foot-tall barnacle- and mussel-encrusted buoy that sits in the middle of the Singapore pavilion at the Venice Biennale.

Another part of *SEA STATE* features looping drone films of sand being endlessly poured into the sea. Speed and slowness are conflated in these aerial shots; they are hypnotic, black sand being poured into turquoise waters, silt slowly disappearing into the water. The view from above allows us just a glimpse of an incomprehensible landscape. When I speak to Lim about his work, he tells me of his childhood in a small fishing village by the sea, Mata Ikan. When the land reclamation projects began, suddenly the sea became farther and farther away, replaced by never-ending dunes of sand. He tells me about the finality of legal proceedings by which Singapore proclaims its ownership of this *terra nova*.

I look at the laws he points me to and am struck by their comprehensive inventory of "corals, stone, clay, sand, gravel, and other natural deposits, brine, petroleum and any other mineral oil or relative hydrocarbon, and natural gas." The Foreshores Act has legal precedents in colonial laws that were enacted in 1872 and then revised by the post-colonial state in the 1980s. Territorial rights. The right to this territory.

—

I see Lim's unmistakable shots of sand again when I watch the Cambodian-American filmmaker Kalyanee Mam's short documentary *Lost World*. In sixteen minutes, my suspicions about reclaimed land and the Gardens are deepened. I learn that Singapore is buying millions of metric tons of sand every year that come from Cambodia's mangrove forests and riverbeds. The environmental consequences of this are manifold and devastating; Cambodia needs the mangroves to protect against erosion, rising sea levels, tsunamis, and hurricanes. Communities need the sand for their ecosystems and lives.

I am from Southeast Asia, but I have never been to Cambodia. Until I went to university in the United States, I had never met anyone from Cambodia. My parents loved to travel, and we had seen the textbook sights in Europe, North America, and Australia, and, in Asia, Thailand, Malaysia, and Japan. But the rest of the region was out of bounds, for reasons that I did not question as I was growing up. I had vague ideas of war, unrest, and violence in these countries, but no more was ever said.

In her accompanying essay to her short film, Mam reorients the way I think about the region I was born in and the sand that it is built on.

> For the wildlife and people of Koh Sralau, the mangrove forests and the sand that roots and grounds these forests are jewels in and of themselves. They are valued for what they are and not for what they could be. The sand is a jewel because it adorns and gives life and sustenance

> to the mangroves and the creatures and the people who have made their home here. Once it is mined and stripped from its home, it loses its luster. It becomes just sand, sterile and lifeless—without a home, without roots, without memory.

The images on the screen open up into a world that is both familiar and unfamiliar. I watch as the Cambodian fisherwoman Phalla Vy and her children carefully negotiate their way through a thicket of mangroves, harvesting snails and clams, foraging. Mam then takes Phalla to Singapore to show her the stockpiles of sand that the country has amassed and the Gardens themselves.

The hand-held camera that follows Phalla through the Cloud Forest conservatory allows us to experience her disorientation in this precisely curated space. Each specific plant in its right place, each drainage pipe, each steel girder, each guided pathway. She cannot read the signs in English, she touches the plants, she places her face into a blossom. She is surrounded by tourists who are taking constant videos and photographs, treating the flora as object and backdrop. The light is so beautiful, refracted as it is through the glass, tempered by the water. Phalla sees the space for exactly what it is. She intones, "If this was real, imagine how beautiful it would be."

At the end of her companion essay to the film, Mam questions the ethics of Singapore's reclaimed lands and their destructive origins, asking:

> What kind of world can be built from sterile and lifeless sand and land that has no roots, no history, and no memory, except for the violent extraction from its homeland? And what kind of world is left behind, when roots, history, and memory have been torn from beneath our feet? It is already enough to be removed from one's land. It is another thing entirely to have one's land removed as well.

I cannot forget the singular scene in the film when Phalla grasps a handful of sand and lets it run through her fingers, an unmistakable echo of Lim's videos of sand being poured into the sea. She believes this is still her land and says she is grieving for it. I think of her presence in the film, dwarfed by the piles of sand, seen as an unwelcome ghost in the Gardens, knowing all the while the cost of this Eden.

Grief

When is a landscape grievable in a history of demolitions and master plans? In a history of the state's constant recalibration of control over its spaces and its bodies?

Does it begin with the first excavation, the felling of the first tree, the first clearing, the first foundation, when the shovel hits that red clay dirt? Do the tears start to fall with evictions, dispossessions, fires that burn down the "slums" and villages for development?

Or perhaps even before that: when the land comes into being. Willed into a colony, a nation, a struggle.

If landscapes are not grievable, then do they ever matter? How are they planned, how do they come to be? Nostalgia becomes a way of retroactively assigning value to the mundane and the banal: a tile design, a brick from the ruins of a library, a nondescript street corner, or an architectural feature. Nostalgia becomes that collection of sepia photographs, transmuted into digital form, slide shows repeated ad nauseam in the institutions of state memory.

Things that can be easily seen, wrapped, purchased, gifted, lost.

I take all my desires for the home-cooked meals, the spices, the plants, fragrant from another climate. I bury them, under the impending snow.

I forget what it might mean for tongue to taste the saltiness, the heat. To think of that specific set of flavours, that palate, a self no longer present, almost forgotten.

What would it be like to always remain in a single place? Never wanting something, somewhere else? My ancestors had little choice, driven by famine, acculturation, and assimilation as survival. The sea in their blood and mine.

—

My older son refuses to continue this journey. He wants to remain in the middle of the country, where he has lived for the past six years. This prairie city, its flatness, its increasing diversity, its wide-open spaces.

"I am the kind of person who wants to live in a place where my kids will know the friends I went to high school with."

A continuity with which I cannot provide him. A bind of familiarity that feels too much like pressure to me.

—

Singapore and Saskatoon are bound together by extraction. They are, in the end, not so different from each other. Outposts of Empire. Members of the Commonwealth. Each at the confluence of land and river, each sitting on Indigenous land that was "ceded" by treaty, each seen as a trophy for the Crown.

Billions of dollars of potash, wheat, semi-chemical wood pulp, and peas make their way from the prairie to the island. In return, Singapore sends vaccines, blood, antisera, toxins, and cultures. It ships heating machinery, integrated circuits, and gas turbines. I imagine these chemicals, foods, materials, bodily fluids, bacterial and viral strains, machines, and chips swirling in a mutable cloud moving across the ocean. I know they must be neatly compacted away in anonymous containers with carefully regulated temperatures, but they cannot be disambiguated.

—

My mother never moved again after she left Malaysia to marry my father and settle in Singapore. By way of an explanation, she said,

"I never wanted to feel like a second-class citizen in another country."

Yet she did not take up Singaporean citizenship, even as it was offered to her. Even as she was an asset to the nation as teacher extraordinaire, care counsellor, pillar of the church.

She was photographed extensively by her foster parents, but never before the age of one. I did not realize why until much later, why my grandmother never discussed her own pregnancy but only my mother's.

As I was growing up, the secrets that surrounded my mother's birth came to me second-hand, implied, disguised.

Some days I wonder whether I am worried about her real parents because she did not seem concerned. I think that if I don't consider these things, then nobody will, and these faceless grandparents, this couple with too many children fleeing the Japanese occupation, will be forever lost.

I am not the only child of an only child, and if I do not remember this, no one will. Everyone out here could be a potential uncle, aunt, cousin. A whole new secret family tree, waiting to stretch out its roots and branches.

—

"I was really skinny and malnourished, my brothers had apparently once left me in a drain."

"You had brothers?"

"Yes, that's what they said."

"Do you remember them?"

"No."

"Haven't you ever wanted to find them?"

"No, not really."

—

Much later, I visit my mother's biological sister. She too has a form of Parkinson's.

She is younger than my mother, their family having reached a point where they could afford to keep their children with them. She tells me of aunts and uncles in China: Shanghai, Xinjiang, other place names I have no way of placing in a geography whose vastness is unfathomable to me.

Our family came from Shanghai, she says, and now they are dispersed. I recall a month spent in that city, where every taxi driver mistook me for Shanghainese, repeating phrases in a language that was wholly unfamiliar to me. Her voice is as quiet as my mother's. She cannot swallow either, and trembles ever so slightly.

What if these neurological failures came from our complex history? What if these synapses became faulty because of these circuits of loss, abandonment, and the stress of forced migration? This restlessness, this unsettlement lodged deep in me.

As for my mother, she had the addition of a complicated gratitude to the couple that adopted her. She did not find out she was not who she was supposed to be until she was twelve.

Tomb

While the Gardens by the Bay are coming into being, Singaporeans stumble upon an old cemetery in the middle of the island. The only reason for this is that the state is about to demolish parts of it to build an eight-lane expressway. I have lived so close to these burial grounds all my life but had never heard of them until I left the island. Bukit Brown is home to the remains of approximately 100,000 people, mostly of the Chinese diaspora, and rainforest plants and birds that are critically endangered.

The Asian fairy bluebird, the chestnut-bellied malkoha, the black-headed bulbul, the banded woodpecker, the orange-bellied flowerpecker, the red-crowned barbet—I have never heard of these birds. If I saw one, I would not be able to recognize or name it.

A scientist painstakingly catalogues the disappearing plants: *Ailanthus integrifolia*, *Anodendron candolleanum*,

Discospermum malaccense, *Hancea penangensis*, *Memecylon paniculatum*, *Microcos tomentosa*, *Piper baccatum*, *Prunus arborea*, *Salacia korthalsiana*, *Trigonachras acuta*, *Xylopia magna*. Embedded in the Latin are place names in the region and an archive of the colonial cataloguing.

I have lived by and amongst these plants all my life, unable to differentiate between them. The tree I remember the most from my childhood is the rubber tree, *Hevea brasiliensis*, first brought to Singapore in 1877 after having been germinated in the Botanic Gardens in London. They were stolen from Brazil, seventy thousand seeds smuggled out by Sir Henry Wickham. This act destroyed livelihoods in Brazil and created a massive class of indentured rubber tappers in British colonies.

All I learned about the plant was from long walks with my father in the reservoir park next to our apartment blocks, as we made a game of hunting together for the stone-like rubber fruits and bringing them home. These mottled, brown, hard-cased pods explode to pollinate the plant, a biotic explosive dehiscence.

As for Bukit Brown, the state moves ahead with its already fixed plans, exhuming over three thousand graves to build the road. It is the living and not the dead that need to be going places, and fast. I have not been to this place. I cannot tell you, really, what holds me back from it. A fear of grief, a fear of loss, a fear of love.

Screen

"Là, tout n'est qu'ordre et beauté,
Luxe, calme et volupté."

—CHARLES BAUDELAIRE, "L'INVITATION AU VOYAGE"

". . . we must expend our limited and slender resources [on those specially endowed future citizens] in order that they will provide that yeast, that ferment, that catalyst in our society which alone will ensure that Singapore shall maintain its pre-eminent place in the societies that exist in South East Asia. . . ."

—LEE KUAN YEW, 1967 SPEECH AT A CONVOCATION DINNER OF THE UNIVERSITY OF SINGAPORE

"Have you ever questioned the nature of your reality?"

—*WESTWORLD*, VARIOUS CHARACTERS

As I watched the third season of the HBO series *Westworld*, my husband kept telling me to keep quiet. I couldn't help myself. Confined to the middle of the North American continent, in its vast, flat, and sparsely populated core, I was unable to stop articulating each moment and space of uncanny familiarity that I saw on the screen. I called out the national art gallery masquerading as a bank, the waterfront park with a fictional helipad, the arts school as high-tech office building, the futuristic fifty-storey public housing development festooned with sky parks, the mass rapid transit station with its sharp architectural lines—all the perfectly clipped and landscaped vistas that Singapore offers up.

The city-state of my birth was rearranged onscreen, its locations subtly adjusted to represent something else with a disorienting dream logic. As I watched this alchemy, I knew my vision was doubled. I saw the sleek fiction of a glossy, dystopian world with its flawless android skin and futuristic architecture and vehicles. Simultaneously, I was immersed in a synesthetic memory of warm tropical nights in the ever-changing city-state. I struggle to describe it to those who have never visited. I try to explain how it's layered with the repressive, mundane, and absurd, how it is always under construction. But perhaps it is a condition of those of us in the diaspora to always be in some form of doubleness, some mode of translation. Perhaps it is only that we feel this more acutely than those still living there. After all, Singapore has always been trying to perform some version of itself, some interpretation that would attract money, capital, labour, tourism, awards—recognition that would assuage its anxiety about its position in the world.

No surprise, then, that the Singapore Tourism Board refused to acknowledge the irony in assisting with the filming of a show that casts the city as a beautiful dystopia. I watched a featurette of the cast who were roped into promoting the city as a tourist destination. I listened to their platitudes about food and architecture, and noted how they stumbled over the production's raison d'être in Singapore:

> LUKE HEMSWORTH: "It's a wonderful place and it parallels the future of *Westworld* really well. There's this shiny exterior to everything, and there is an undercurrent as well."
>
> INTERVIEWER: "How did you think it played well into the *Westworld* scenario?"
>
> HEMSWORTH: "Not that Singapore is like this, but obviously the future of *Westworld* is glistening on the outside but underneath it is quite toxic."

In another clip, the showrunners Jonathan Nolan and Lisa Joy lauded the "future" as depicted by Singapore and softened by the verdant greenery. The clever art of camouflage that the city excels in. They praised its soft curves and decadent delights, and were captivated by its deliberate, well-managed nature—yet part of the season depicts a riot staged in a similar setting, hinting at the repressed impulses that run deep.

—

Joshua Comaroff and Ong Ker-Shing write about the phenomenon of "paramilitary gardening" in Singapore—of landscaping as a kind of urban warfare against the populace. Their essay begins with a photograph of masked workers protecting themselves against grass clippings and the heat, wielding electric scythes and cutters. Going to battle.

> The landscapers are in charge here. And in a very muscular way. This city-state has quite literally been hacked from voracious equatorial forest; its geo-body has been "reclaimed" from the sea, fogged and trimmed and cooled in submission.

It takes inconceivable amounts of work to keep this tropicality in check, to groom and shape the plants into submission. I try to comprehend the planning, the man-hours, human time and effort. I imagine the repetitive strain that must be part of that back-breaking crouching, cutting, weeding, trimming. That increasing heat and humidity that makes you long for a burst of cool relief.

I remember, as well, Tan Pin Pin's meditative film *In Time to Come*, which features her quiet, persistent gaze at the repetitions and rituals that make up the banal progress that we name as Singapore. In one scene, the camera does not flinch as workers dismember and cut down a forty-year-old banyan tree that was emblematic of the alternative arts venue it sheltered. Members of the arts community look on with grief and disbelief as, limb by limb, the enormous tree is taken apart. A section is loaded onto a vehicle, to be perhaps revived at a later date. The tree harboured memories of the changes in the city, but had grown large and spontaneous, permanently damaging a building wall.

—

I couldn't help but love the Singapore I saw onscreen. Was it familiarity or nostalgia that made me so susceptible? I could not tear myself away from the glass, the steel, concrete, neon, and green. I could almost feel the warmth of that equatorial night. In the first few episodes of the season, I was fine with understanding that Singapore was supposed to stand in for Los Angeles of the future. That this slick American creation was employing the time-honoured, if Orientalist, mode of using the exotic other as a cautionary yet seductive future.

So I was a little surprised when, in the middle of the season, the most distinctive elements of the city's skyline featured as an exterior shot. The Esplanade, a "world-class art venue" destined to play host to the city's globalized artistic aspirations. The dome lit gold, glowing smugly. The interior of the dome was some other luxe bar in Singapore, entirely different, but I was willing to suspend my disbelief. A sleight of hand.

> MAEVE: "Another simulation? Well, this one's a bit over the top."
>
> SERAC: "No, Maeve. This is Singapore."

I gasped. Singapore was finally playing itself.

The season's main plot line revolves around Engerraund Serac, a secretive, authoritarian figure who we find out has surrendered his voice and agency to a supercomputer, an algorithm that seeks order and predictability for the human race at all costs. The parallels one might draw with the all-pervasive Master Plan in Singapore and its soft authoritarian government are dizzying. As I trawled the internet for images of Vincent

Cassel, the actor who plays Serac, I hesitated on one that shows him all dressed in a light shade of cream. Where had I seen that carefully coiffed grey hair, that penchant for white clothing? Eyes with their indomitable expression of power?

I am aware, of course, of the dangers of over-reading. The acts of recognition that I was engaged in as I watched the show, naming the iconic buildings and vistas, led to a strange dissonance for me. One that I am assuming the showrunners were attempting to induce: that deep underlying sense of unease amidst all this luxury, order, and pleasure—an island the equivalent of the decadent but ordered fantasy that Charles Baudelaire describes in his invitation to a voyage: "There, all is order and beauty / luxury, peace, and pleasure." His cynical poem, damning in its repetition of *"Luxe, calme et volupté."*

—

What underpins Singapore's shiny success? In the show, the plight of those condemned to do menial work or petty crime is focalized through the character of Caleb, played by the American everyman Aaron Paul. Since the algorithms predict Caleb's eventual suicide, he is discouraged from procreating. In the future depicted by *Westworld*, someone like him would never be socially mobile. This is reflected in his physical mobility through

Los Angeles/Singapore: Unlike the privileged class who navigate and view the city through helicopters, Caleb trawls the subway systems and back alleys of future Los Angeles. There are riots when those like him become enraged at the planned future that awaits them, or at least what the algorithm predicts.

In a 1967 speech at a convocation dinner for new graduates from the University of Singapore, Prime Minister Lee Kuan Yew mused about when one "should assess the quality of a boy or girl" to "make a realistic assessment of his intellectual and his physical potentials . . . in order to cultivate to maximum fruition whatever qualities he has for best performance and fruition." Just two years after Singapore's independence, Lee began calculating the percentages and numbers of those "who are more than ordinarily endowed physically and mentally." He concluded that, at this early point in the nation's trajectory, "there will be some 3,000 specially endowed future citizens," though perhaps this number must be multiplied by two "in order to be quite safe that we have not left out somebody who really has these gifts."

It seems impossible not to draw a line from the implications of this speech to the generations of children and parents fixating on the PSLE (Primary School Leaving Examination), the annual national standardized exam that determines the path, or "stream," of a child.

Were they qualified to be Special, Express, or Normal? Were they Normal (Academic) or Normal (Technical)? In the years when policy-makers decided to change the scoring systems, crises erupted in the national conversation. Some families, cognizant of the stakes of this sorting mechanism in a tightly competitive country, devoted years of their lives to ensuring that their children had the best chances of obtaining a good score. The mathematics problems were so notoriously difficult that they were often reproduced in the newspapers, with adults racking their brains over questions about rolls of ribbons, distances between libraries and bakeries, distributing chocolates, percentages of grey triangles, and arrangements of semicircles.

I remember answering innumerable practice questions compiled from previous examinations. As the exam dates got closer and closer, it felt as if we were all standing on the edge of a precipice. We forgot what it felt like to be twelve. We knew that to be "Normal" was a disappointment. The word itself became a category, a stream that would mark you for years and years to come. We wanted the upward mobility that would come with being "Express," and perhaps some of us even dreamt of being "Special."

But the state didn't want to just stop at "streams"; it wanted to reach back much further in the ever more precise management of excellence. In his study

"Eugenics on the Rise: A Report from Singapore," C.K. Chan notes how

> the Singapore technocracy . . . has repeatedly shown itself quite willing and capable of undertaking those measures which it believes to be in the long-term interest and viability of the system as a whole. . . . [T]he introduction of the eugenic measures, for the social planners, merely expresses a concern that the "quality" of the Singaporean population measures up to the demands of an advanced, highly technological society.

Chan observes how the most famous articulation of these policies came in 1983, when Lee gave a controversial speech during the country's annual National Day Rally. Archival footage shows a roomful of rapt attendees fanning themselves and melting in the tropical heat. In his characteristic pause-filled style, the old man makes his pronouncements on the dismal state of the reproductive rate of educated women. He calls for measures to suppress the birth rates of the lowly educated while finding ways to provide incentives for graduate women to settle down and marry while still in their prime. I listen to the rapturous applause from the audience.

I think of the meticulous compilation of statistics that Lee uses to bolster his argument. The army of faceless civil servants that collected this data and extrapolated biopolitical policy from it. One of the tactics to encourage more children results in a public ad campaign with slogans like "Why not reality? You could wait a lifetime for a dream" and "Are you giving men the wrong idea?" I think about how control and planning extend into beds, bodies, hearts. How we are encouraged to relive and reproduce these loops of school, army, work, and family. The carefully planned housing-development-board estates with their town centres and amenities. The batches of fresh recruits marching off to their compulsory months of basic military training with their standard-issue backpacks and fatigues. Some are shunted off to the police and firefighting services, since Lee decided their loyalties would be torn if war was waged against our regional neighbours. The rest trudge in forests as infantrymen or undergo elite training to be officers, commandos. I think about the routes we take.

In the introduction to her book *This Is What Inequality Looks Like*, the sociologist Teo You Yenn includes a hand-drawn diagram of the circumscribed world of her lower-income interviewees: the locations of market, post office, school, bank, and home are marked out with arrows denoting travel between these limited sites. She notes how their lives are confined to a radius of a few kilometres, unlike the lives of the middle and upper classes, whose status symbols include frequent transnational tours and trips. Their lives are very much like those of the rich as depicted in *Westworld*, looking for the next thrill, the next expensive fix. Teo writes, "Mobility/immobility are lived realities as well as imagined states of being. They describe our everyday movements. And they shape how we think about where we have been and where we can still go." She asks, "What of those who have, within the structure of this narrative, stood still?" And I think, what if they have been made to stand still? What if they have had all their lives decided for them and never thought to question the nature of their reality?

—

Even as I watched this iteration of Singapore unfold onscreen, another version, taken hold of by the pandemic, was unravelling online. In this exceptional time, the vast inequalities of the system that I'd left were clarified. At first lauded for its gold-standard pandemic control, the island finally succumbed to its open secret: the immense underclass of foreign workers, the enforced poverty and apartheid-like living conditions that sustain the unsustainable.

They quarantined tens of thousands of men, even as their tight quarters meant that infections raged through their dormitories. They mandated that the domestic workers stay in even on their hard-earned days off. I peered at the men's living conditions through grainy online videos. I, like so many others, tracked the inadequate meals that were delivered to them in a country where it is possible to eat lavishly with rare and expensive ingredients shipped from any part of the world. There were stark photographs of plain rice, two pieces of curried okra, and a small portion of indeterminate protein. Some of the men refused to eat. Numerous others were sickened by the disease. They slept fifteen to twenty to a room. Those who were ill were taken away, not to return. One account describes how they were never told whether their tests were positive or negative. When some of them died of heart attacks, their deaths were not recorded as part of the toll from the virus. A column appeared in the state newspaper suggesting that these workers be housed on floating platforms to better maximize the value of the land. The police sent in all-terrain autonomous robots to help maintain safe distancing in the dormitories. I could no longer tell the difference between speculative fiction and reality.

—

> LIAM DEMPSEY JR.: "It almost looks like it makes sense from up here. All you see is the order of it, the plan."

One of the central tropes in *Westworld* is to blur that classic binary between fantasy and reality, artifice and performance versus the real and the lived. Are the robots more human than human? Are the humans much like subjects caught in simulated loops? Decades of a Master Plan for both inhabitants and urban planning in Singapore have produced a carefully calibrated social, political, and spatial order. A fiction and vision made material, concealed by imported greenery. Singapore's relation to the unreal and artificial is no clearer than its now-ideal status for numerous photo shoots and luxe film sets. The city-state has always had this powerful need to be seen, to be recognized, to be lauded as a seamless, smooth, globalized cityscape and skyline.

The ways in which the show amalgamates downtown Los Angeles with Singapore, blending the two cities and then adding previously imagined buildings that were never built—courtesy of the production designer Howard Cummings and the Danish architect Bjarke Ingels—point to how Singapore's cityscape exists as aspirational fiction and fancy. I am reminded of the work of the photographer and conceptual artist Robert Zhao Renhui. His work *The Land Archive: Singapore 1925–2025* comprises numerous photographs that purport to be part of this fictional archive. These composite images capture a city that flickers between dream and reality. They document the skyscrapers that seem to arise overnight, the instant trees, and the fertilized, manicured, tightly controlled greenery. Each of Zhao's photographs is undated, miring the work in indeterminate time, the time of the simulation. Sand dunes appear in incongruous places, as do wild animals, massive, long-dead trees, hills that have little to do with the current topography of the island, a single human figure in a flood of water trying to extricate his motorcycle. The surreal, the illusory, the cautionary. One photograph entitled "View of Marina Bay Sands" is, as Zhao puts it, "a scene that will never happen . . . a composite of two cities from Japan and the United Kingdom, two countries which have shaped how our island looks today."

All of this land has never been ours, is stolen, occupied, carved out, and reclaimed—sand seized from the hills, the islands, the river deltas. In the face of patriotic songs, strict rules surrounding how and when flags can be displayed, and manufactured zeal, Zhao's work asks difficult questions about Singapore's ecological pasts and futures. How we take for granted all that we can see, which often hides what we refuse to acknowledge. To face the complicated truth of this island in its totality, with its missteps, contradictions, and paradoxes, would be to truly recognize the labour, the hands that built all of this—convict labour, indentured labour, the dispensable bodies eaten up by the grinding machinery. Looking at a photograph like "View of Marina Bay Sands" sets our vision akilter, forces us out of a familiar view, breaks open the illusion of this city, built to impress, the country as backdrop.

—

For the moment, I cannot return to the country of my birth. My father bluntly points out, in a blurry video call, that even if I wanted to return for a familial funeral or rite, the strict quarantine period that I would have to observe would mean I would find myself belated, too late. But I can continue to watch the city as it is filtered through my screen, distorted, truth-telling, sometimes more immediate than I care for.

The digital images I peruse every day now are self-conscious of their depiction of the abnormal, the uncanny. All I have are these vistas, mediated through screens large and small. The sheen of bright lights on Thandie Newton's face. The empty bus stops, with their alternate seats crossed out by coloured tape. The tropical, chic, modernist architecture of the new downtown. The wildness of the fields next to the orderly rows of flats. The gleaming, climate-controlled airport with its rows and rows of luggage trolleys, its expanse, completely empty. The public parks patrolled by robot dogs. Communal spaces and seating designated by cordons and stickers with various injunctions. Barriers and regulations now made visible.

How many ways can one see one's homeland? I hear that the construction sites have gone silent, the grass overgrown, the native flowers and plants returned, grown shin-deep, blossomed, taking back the space. I wish I could be there to see it.

Cut

At nineteen, I did not believe in the next twenty-one years. A figure still, remote, and abstract. Over the next few years, mastering my hypochondria and pessimism, I read all the studies of stunted growth, early-onset dementia, failing cardiovascular systems; death, premature.

My mother wept when she looked at the X-ray. My anomaly that exceeded the bounds of a pelvic ultrasound.

She said, "It's my fault."

Did she count backwards to some unknown failure in the matrilineal line? An ancestor, carrying the gene that would lead to my body's malfunction? Or did she consider each action that she had taken, each contaminated environment, some errant chemical, unperceived, absorbed into her body or mine?

I didn't cry. I looked coolly, detached, at the X-ray films, their hardy emulsion-gelatin, radiation-sensitive silver bromide illuminating my insides.

Later there would be a blank in the wink between counting down, blacking out, and being called awake again.

My surgeon smiled proudly to himself as he removed the gauze in one swift movement. Clean, surgical wounds, see? I noted the carefully placed scar he gave me, running from hip to hip. It endures to this day, a length of imperfection that has roped into something weaker and stronger at the same time.

I gazed up into his smooth, unlined face. I had put my days in his hands, my hours, my years. He used words like *occluded* and *worry*; he used words like *confirmation* and *chance*. He asked me about my marriage prospects. I wondered how he kept track of all of us, all of our lives. He told me I was young, and I realized that I needed to be reminded of this.

—

I lay in a darkened room, one without windows.

Is everything all right?

No, there seems to be a recurrence.

I was tired of recurring. Of the perpetual routines of scans. An unmentionable "woman's thing," as an acquaintance once referred to it, both brushing it off and clouding it in shame.

Removing clothes. Sitting on newly changed rolls of paper covering nondescript beds. The sticky, warm gel across my pelvis and between my legs. The fear that came before and after.

—

A week after the first surgery I was given the biopsy report, including a photograph of what they had removed from me. It didn't look as though it belonged to me. I remember lying in my bed the night before the procedure and gingerly feeling my abdomen. How could I never have noticed this foreignness just below my rib cage, between my hips? It had grown so large.

Another time, I was immediately given digital stills from my procedure, filmed during the laparoscopy. The first time you see the inside of your body, you immediately recoil from the colours, the blood, the alien nature of what is just beneath the surface, under your epidermis. But this is me, somehow more me than my hair or skin or eyes, this is me within me. Teratoma, *teratos*, the Greek word for monster.

—

What I remember most, however indistinctly, are the transitions to and from consciousness.

Transitions from where my body was in the hands of careful strangers to where I began to breathe independently, to remembering how my limbs worked, and to listening to instructions.

The anesthesiologist telling me not to look at the needle moving the drug into my vein. Closing my eyes, opening myself up to the dark, red flowers pooling in front of my eyes, drawing me again into an unknown.

A nurse's voice, telling me it was time to wake up, as if all I had next was a day of school.

An oxygen mask placed over my face, the damp plastic pressing against my cheeks, the space between my eyes, dipping below my chin.

Breathe.

Even as I was too tired to make my lungs obey; all I wanted was more of this dreamless sleep.

—

"You're a fighter," my father says, a decade later. He reminds me again of my mother's miscarriages. I'm the one that made it.

—

For a long while after my first ovarian surgery, I am so afraid of what I can and cannot put into my body.

I scrutinize the world around me with new eyes. What caused this defect, this misfiring on a cellular level? I become briefly obsessed with hydroponic salad, as if I seek to eat only things that have not touched this land, this soil.

My grandmother, with her insistent and instinctual distinctions between what is clean and what is dirty, what is pure and what is contaminated, does not seem so pathological anymore. My body is porous, to the dust, the roads, the oil refineries, the industrial food complex that my father works in. How could anyone be surprised at this outcome?

When my grandmother comes to the end of her long life, after surviving her husband and every one of her siblings, she looks down at what is left as I am bathing her. She has been so healthy for so long, so careful in her choices, so dreadfully difficult in her ways. And yet she notes her fragile skin covering her even more delicate blood vessels and says that nothing is recognizable.

Heel

"Let's try that again."

I'm in a small, black-walled studio—a rehearsal space for the real thing. I place my foot on the teleprompter. If I press the ball of my foot down, the text scrolls down. If I push my heel down, the text on the monitor above the camera reverses its flow. I can control how fast or how slow I want to read by calibrating the minute differences in pressure that my foot exerts.

"Let's try that again, but this time I want you to remember to pause."

I'm being trained to read the news. How to arrange my face in a perfectly neutral yet friendly way, even without smiling. It's an expression that, once mastered, is difficult to lose. I study the tapes of my predecessors, absorbing the correct methods—screen to eye to brain to cheek muscles.

Widen your eyes slightly to convey interest and attentiveness.

Purse your lips ever so slightly to indicate a readiness to reply.

Tilt your head the tiniest angle down and to the left and then move it again up and to the right.

Hold that expression for three seconds before the news clip you have introduced begins to play.

Pressure

The first time someone who is not a lover puts their full weight on you is a revelation. The pressure on your spine and neck. Each cervical nerve bracing against your spinal column, bearing another's weight.

Before stepping on the mat, you bow. You touch your partner's fingertips, their fists. You bend your body at the hips, hold up your hands in front of your face in a fighting stance. You circle warily, you feint, you move to grab the lapel and the sleeve. Instead of pushing your partner away, you pull her towards you as you put one foot on her hip. You sit down as you do this and put your legs around her waist.

A dance.

—

"Stop writing that email and go to the editor's office."

I look up from my desk dinner—lukewarm rice, vegetables, and fried luncheon ham. These are long days and we often choose from the leftovers at the office cafeteria, sit in front of our computers jamming food into our mouths as we push out our stories for the night news. I have worked in the bowels of Singapore's state-controlled media for two years now. Enough of the tasks and procedures that I do have become so routine that I hardly bother to really think about what it is I am actually writing. The network is called Channel NewsAsia, even as the country hasn't always wanted to be associated with the rest of the region.

"I said stop what you're doing and come with me."

My editor, a tall, unnervingly soft-spoken man, repeats his demand.

I close the Styrofoam box that holds the remains of my meal and lock my computer screen before getting up to follow him to the head editor's office.

Opening the frosted glass–panelled door, I see that she is livid.

"How stupid are you?"

She repeats this statement twice, once in low tones and another time screaming for the benefit of the rest of the office. She jabs a finger into the air near my head for emphasis.

Through her rage, I smell her fear.

We are not supposed to contradict members of the government. We are not supposed to hold email arguments with these men. And certainly, someone as junior as me should not have disagreed with a minister, should not even have had an opinion in the first place.

"You'll never get anywhere if I have anything to say about it."

I imagine the filaments of power and influence uncurling from her slim, manicured fingers. I look carefully at her face, scarred as it is from a childhood accident, and now incandescent with her rage. The uneven, bark-like skin on her face a testimony to what happens when you stand too close to a flame.

—

You have to remember the steps to escape a mount. Wait for the smallest opening. The gap in which your opponent relaxes her grip on your wrists for just an instant. Later there will be bruises, but for now your body is so full of waiting that this barely registers. Wait for the gap, then destabilize her centre of gravity, grab the sleeve of one hand, and push her over to her side. Begin again.

—

I remember growing up with whispered conversations, worried glances over shoulders. Even now, I have acquaintances who turn their phone to airplane mode before opening their mouths.

When you live in a police state, it is not only that the actual police wield immense amounts of power. It is that everyone is a part of this state. Everyone polices.

No one tells you explicitly what you're policing against.

But you know.

No system can be total. No hold can last forever; there are always gaps. Even in the confines of our small island state, there are pockets of possible resistance.

But more and more I wonder if these gaps, these hatches, are simply safety valves permitted by the state, to carefully regulate its mechanisms, its organisms.

A poem here, a play there, a piece of rogue performance art, a snatch of conversation in a coffee shop, in a taxicab, a bit of digital chatter, a sliver of code. Or, even, the pleasures of eating well or the fleeting nostalgia for a demolished library, contained in a leftover brick sold at the new library's gift shop.

What are these trivialities in the face of the state? In the body of the state?

—

Sometimes, I forget the weight of power. It is so easy to be seduced by the cool, climate-controlled glass corridors, the tropical light without heat. This is possible if I forget what was here before these new glass buildings, their concrete foundations digging deep into the soft red earth.

Sometimes, in between interviews and piece-to-cameras, I inhale sharply: that new-building smell. Always fresh paint, newly welded metal, new concrete, cut wires, unbelievably clean carpet. I stand, leaning against a new metal-girded pillar, feel its coldness cut through my polyester blazer, against my spine.

Sometimes, for the sake of "heritage" and "progress," new glass and steel extensions are simply melded into an older building. A supreme court becomes an art gallery. An old house becomes a small front to an office building. Controlling this architectural version of history means that the state controls our futures in these spaces as well: how we move in them, how we breathe in them, how the light shapes our skin. This is not preservation—just another form of control.

—

Sometimes your escape doesn't work. You stay pinned down. Those holds on your wrists will bloom into contusions dark blue and purple.

You learn to be patient. You learn to stop fighting. You learn to wait. No one can keep this hold on you forever. If they hold on to your wrists, they cannot choke you.

You are at an impasse.

—

I sit in the passenger seat of the news van exchanging pleasantries with the camera crew. Some of them are wizened, weather-beaten, shoulders askew from bearing their hefty gear.

They treat me like a daughter, granddaughter, or beloved niece. They call me "little sister," and as we wend our way through the island, they stop occasionally to buy me treats wrapped in brown paper or packed in plastic containers: a mess of noodles in coriander sauce, sweet, glutinous pastries made by an elderly couple in a hidden shop, milky fish soup infused with ginger and cilantro.

When we tail ministers or members of Parliament in their tours of the orderly housing estates, I buy the crew little plastic bags of milky tea or coffee. These drinks are always too sweet and too bitter at the same time. We wait interminably to place a microphone in front of the mouths of these men. I hold our microphones in a crush of others like me. Painted, mascaraed, sweaty in the torpor.

They speak; we record, faithfully transcribe. We edit only for clarity.

The snacks at the end of each event fuel our compliance. We do this over and over again.

We work night shifts, on weekends, public holidays. I learn to hold a microphone in one hand and a tape recorder in the other. I start to transcribe in the van, listening to their speeches on my headphones, carving out their sound bites, feeding these back to the station even before I return. An efficient conduit.

—

We are hemmed in by the people on the streets. We have never seen people on the streets like this here. We are taught that people on the streets are dangerous—they might assemble, organize, riot. People on the streets happen in other countries, other climates, other nations on our screens. Yet tonight there are bodies all around us, moving as if in unison.

An opposition candidate, Chiam See Tong, has held on to the only seat that a dissenting party has in Parliament, and the people in his ward have taken to the streets in a brief, joyous, anarchic celebration. He has held this seat for more than two decades and against all odds. In recognition of this feat, of their own stubbornness, really, the people come pouring out of the stairwells and corridors. In the humid tropical night, their faces jubilant under the ubiquitous orange street lamps, they bring traffic to a standstill. Hundreds, thousands stream out of the tidy blocks of flats. Car horns sound. There is cheering.

We are disoriented, and I can see the confusion in my colleagues' faces, even the ones who have spent long decades balancing their machines on one shoulder and then the other, eye to the lens, faithfully recording the nation's history and the politicians' banality.

This is an old, defiant ward. Potong Pasir, it is called; "cut sand" in Malay for its colonial history as the site of numerous sand quarries. Its refusal to disavow the lone dissenting voice in Parliament clearly punished with its aging elevators, peeling paint, and the chipped concrete of its high-rise blocks. Each nick and imperfection a sign of a space bypassed in the nation's march of progress. There is a certain makeshift quality to any improvements that have been made. Improvisations to make the living easier. The grass is just a little overgrown, the trees just a little under-pruned—little errors in the overall algorithm of our island life.

We are pushed through the streets. My crew stays close to me because we aren't popular here, after all. Bits of state machinery in a part of the state that is in open revolt, refusing to slip into the proper gear.

"Hey! I bet you aren't going to film this!"

A high-spirited youth taunts us with an obscene gesture before sprinting away to catch up with his friends. They return as a group, hamming it up for a camera that—he's right—isn't recording. We know that even if we let the tape roll, there is no way an editor would approve this footage. There is too much glee here, giddiness almost.

With great difficulty, we make it back to the live feed point. We dutifully file the report. We wait for our slot in the news cycle. We frame the shot, carefully hiding the magnitude of the crowd on the streets. We do this wordlessly, because after months, years of this work, we know, without knowing how, what he wants. I wait for the lights to be angled properly on my face. I wait, holding the microphone, ignoring the crowd and watching for the red light of the camera to blink on next to its eye. I wait for my cue.

—

There is an increasing complexity to the submissions that you are learning.

"The arm has to be held straight, the thumb pointing up. Otherwise, you won't be able to inflict any pain."

When you are caught in an arm lock, you learn how to master your panic. Carefully, your partner begins to straighten your arm beyond its ability. The only way to stop her from breaking you is to tap her side with your free hand.

Tap twice, quickly, and the pressure stops.

“All right, now it’s your turn.”

Quarantine

It was the middle of 2021 before I was able to return to Singapore again. Transiting through the usually busy Tokyo airport, sitting on a plane with just two other passengers, it seemed as though the world would never go back to the way it was before. Upon our arrival at Changi, we were greeted by a phalanx of staff, masked and gowned. We were treated gingerly, channelled into queues in the arrivals hall. I submitted to the first of many COVID tests, putting my head back as far as it would go, listening to the muffled tones of the gentle nurse. With typical efficiency, I was given two colour-coded stickers and shuffled into a large bus. We were not told where we were being taken until the very last moment, when the bus pulled into the driveway of a downtown hotel.

Arriving in my room, I pulled open the floor-to-ceiling curtains in my quarantine hotel to a vertiginous night view. Laid out in front of my bleary eyes after twenty-six hours of travel was an urban panorama both known and new—of ever-changing, reclaimed coastlands, the hotel-casino-shopping complex Marina Bay Sands, the eco-development Gardens by the Bay, the new downtown's glassy skyscrapers around an artificial cove, the carefully preserved colonial architecture, all set against glowing oil tankers and refineries. I was home, surely, or at least confronted with its most ostentatious version of itself.

I had come from the flatness of the North American prairies and eighteen long months of living in a single-storey bungalow built around the same time Singapore declared its independence, in the 1960s. Returning as a prodigal daughter, it was hard not to be dazzled by the planned vista—decades of the Singapore Master Plan attempting to defy intensifying weather patterns, rising sea levels, water scarcity, biodiversity extinction, the vagaries of the financial markets. The engineered solutions to these were in the terraformed former intertidal zones that revealed their multi-faceted character from the perfect vantage point that I had.

As the days passed on the sixty-second floor of what used to be Asia's tallest hotel, time seemed to take on a different quality. I opened the balcony window each morning to take in the dawn light. I watched as the storm clouds raced across the sky, over the meticulously wrought skyline, darkening the faraway asphalt. I cocooned myself in the air-conditioned room in the noontimes when the humidity made the outside air unbearable. The only humans I saw were tiny figures walking, running, or cycling. I caught glimpses of the hotel staff geared up in full personal protective equipment as they delivered food and other necessities to my door. Loved ones sent treats: tropical fruit, favourite dishes, bottled cocktails. The standard meals arrived in the same black plastic containers, each food separated from the others, a menu that repeated every seven days.

Friends texted to tell me to pay attention to the highly choreographed rehearsals for the National Day celebrations in August, which were to take place right in front of my hotel, on a floating platform on the bay. Right until they were abruptly halted due to a sudden spike in COVID-19 cases in the country, my nightly soundtrack was the deafening repetition of soaring patriotic ballads, military band music, and the sharp shocks of gun salutes being practised for accuracy. These sounds echoed and reverberated across the bay and its surrounding buildings, far away and too close all at once. I watched the rehearsed light displays, mass dances, and fireworks, all seemingly in miniature. I watched as, at almost eye level, Chinook helicopters flew the national flag in tight formation in front of my balcony. One afternoon, I felt the building and my own body vibrate from the sonic boom as F-15SG fighter jets flew overhead in synchronized trajectories meant to signify "our collective strength, resolve and unity." The part celebration, part military display felt fitting, a reminder of violence amidst the songs and pageantry. These dress rehearsals are repeated week after week every July, just so everything goes off without a single mistake.

When I was finally free, notified by a terse phone call that my sixth COVID test in sixteen days was unsurprisingly negative, I was released into a city that was quarantining itself. Cordons directed its inhabitants to the correct routes, and painstakingly placed, colourful tape designated where they should and should not sit or stand. Most notably, there was a sophisticated Bluetooth app pinging each person's proximity to another and allowing them to "check in" to every indoor space, indicating where everyone was on the small island. Trace Together. Everyone moved towards each checkpoint with a rote tiredness, holding out their phone to hear that familiar beep and see the green light that would let them pass. Some had refused to download the app, opting for a physical token instead, perhaps somehow imagining this would be less of an intrusion on their privacy.

But what was private anymore? The expansive vision that my quarantine perch had allowed me belied the constrained reality of how the island felt with its external and internal boundaries so tightly maintained. It was as if every rule and injunction against public assembly was suddenly manifest; the pandemic had made every barrier, every inequity starker and more visible.

I couldn't decide whether it was fear or relief that I felt as I spent my days in my childhood apartment and its environs. I took refuge in the reservoir park that had been constructed in the nineteenth century and named after the English engineer who had designed it to provide water for the burgeoning colony. Primary forest mingled with remnants of plantation trees. I took long walks with friends. They told me the island had never felt smaller than in the past year and a half, as they were unable to leave. Each patch of green ground had been traipsed over so many times, each park and outdoor recreational space flooded with crowds keen to leave their small flats. Thousands mourned and fought over the last refuges of wild land that were slated for destruction under the Master Plan to build more flats, more shopping centres, more roads. Yet we did not stray from the designated paths and walkways intended to keep us out of and apart from the delicate ecosystems of the designated water catchment areas, the liquid green heart of the isle.

Bullet

"We give our bombs a full medical."

—CHARTERED INDUSTRIES OF SINGAPORE ADVERTISEMENT

"You can spend a lifetime stitching people up."

—DR. ANG SWEE CHAI

"Better weapons make things difficult."

—*WAR SURGERY FIELD MANUAL*

The caption of a photograph from the National Archives of Singapore reads, "A Chartered Industries of Singapore employee is shown inspecting 5.56mm rounds coming off a production line in 1968." The worker is a young man wearing a blue factory uniform and a pair of white gloves to handle the ammunition. The bullets are spilling off the production line: small, shiny, stubby, gold, cylindrical. Soon, they will be shipped to the Australian troops in Vietnam, five million rounds of 5.56 ammunition. Soon, many of them will find their way into the bodies of men, women, and children. Some lodged in death or in a different kind of life.

—

In starting Singapore's first weapons factory, civil servants were told that not only did the country need a reliable domestic supply of ammunitions and weapons, but also, that they had to make the Chartered Industries of Singapore as profitable as possible to justify its existence. It strikes me that perhaps no one questioned where these profits were going to come from. Perhaps these considerations were irrelevant to a nation that has always felt it was under siege.

Here is another facet of the history of my erstwhile country about which I had grown up knowing nothing. The island is afloat on a sea of bullets, missiles, ammunition, howitzers, automatic rifles, awash in killing. But it was never our fingers on these triggers.

Like any commodity, weapons must be marketed to the consumer. Conflating the language of the country's burgeoning tourism business, one ad reads: "Surprising shots of Singapore." A set of photographs is scattered across the page as if they are postcards of a holiday. Except here, they are filled with images of munitions, charges, bullets, bombs of every size—"Singapore never ceases to surprise."

Working my way through this archive, I find the words "BIG BANG" emblazoned over the top of a two-page spread. It is for a howitzer gun, the FH-88. I wonder what the men behind the ad mean when they say "you'll get more than you bargained for" with the gun's "firepower, mobility and battlefield survivability." What bargain have we struck? I don't understand the details, but "a burst rate of 3 rounds under 15 seconds" and "accuracy to within 0.22% in range and 0.035% in azimuth" clarifies any notion of where these bullets might end up. Who is on the opposite end of this weapon?

There are other iterations of this campaign that note how Chartered Industries of Singapore "just keep[s] growing" as part of the meteoric rise of Singapore's economy. A line of ammunition is laid out across the two pages, from the smallest bullet to a five-hundred-pound aerial bomb. The photograph is pleasing to the eye, sorted as the ammunition is by size. Some are painted a cheery yellow or red at their tips, some gleam gold or bronze. They could be pencils, crayons, pens. The way one writes their legacy into the world.

—

Right after its separation from Malaysia, coming into its own independence, Singapore's new government realized that it must have an army. I have always grown up with the knowledge that mandatory conscription is a given for the boys and men in my life, from my twin uncles to my two sons.

When we move away from Singapore, I painstakingly work through the layers of paperwork and bureaucracy that will grant my sons the permits to exit the country as boys above thirteen years of age, and to defer their enlistment in the military, pending their renunciation of their Singaporean citizenship. The entire process is shrouded, opaque; there are no online forms available as there are for every other small detail in Singaporean life. There are forums of worried parents (mostly mothers) who agonize over whether they left the country soon enough, whether they contacted the correct government department, whether they made some inadvertent mistake by accepting a monetary bonus for bearing a child for the state.

It has been drilled into all of us, the importance of national defence in a state under siege, although from whom is never explicitly stated. I find out that the nascent Singapore Armed Forces owe a great debt to the Israeli Defense Forces, whose representatives worked intensively with Dr. Goh Keng Swee, the country's first minister of defence, to plan and build its fledging military. The details of this relationship find their way into the Israeli press and an academic anthology entitled *Beating the Odds: 50 Years of Singapore-Israel Ties*. There is even a logo that melds the Singapore Merlion with the Star of David. Relations between the two countries are called "a deep, dark love affair."

At the time, it was considered politically dangerous to reveal that the Singapore government had sought aid from the Israelis, so they were called the "Mexicans." Lee Kuan Yew noted that they were "swarthy enough." He told them, "I want you to recruit the most primitive people in the country, the uneducated and the jobless."

—

It would be impossible for me to access any comprehensive government archives of this time in the country's history. In an official photograph of the period, Dr. Goh is in a rain poncho and dress loafers inspecting would-be soldiers in the jungle. These are thin, wiry young men, dressed in singlets, some barefoot. They are standing ramrod straight, a forced posture, their faces expressionless and their gazes unwavering.

There are rumours and small details that are revealed to me, stories that involve my own paternal grandfather. He had been transferred briefly to the Ministry of Defence from the Ministry of Culture to work with the Israelis as they were helping to build Singapore's first army. My father tells me that he never talked about his work there, he couldn't. Instead, he drank heavily and would drive his car back from work down the unpaved rural roads late at night. My father, a boy, would stand at the gate waiting to see the car's headlights shining their shaky way towards the house.

He tells me that my grandfather held the keys to a vault containing important documents. My father remembers army officers arriving in a jeep to retrieve the keys even late at night or on the weekends.

My grandfather was unhappy at this posting, for reasons that will never be known to me. When his term at the ministry was up for renewal, he requested that he be moved to the Ministry of Education instead. I do not have many clear memories of him, just my inheritance of his large ears and perhaps other genetic traits. A persistent refusal to conform, to be complicit, and, paradoxically, the knowledge that one can never not be complicit.

—

In her book *From Beirut to Jerusalem*, the dissident Singaporean surgeon Ang Swee Chai reproduces a letter she wrote to her husband Francis Khoo during the Sabra and Shatila massacres in the early eighties in Lebanon:

> Darling, we are just two tiny individuals in this tide of historical liberation. Somewhere we may be washed away, forming the error margin—washed aside—but we know where the tide will flow, and nothing can stop it. It may sound rhetorical—but in the whole history of the oppressed people struggling for justice, nothing will ever sound rhetorical enough.

I have never heard this language from a Singaporean before. Her letter to Francis leaves me speechless. Her love for him, her commitment to justice, her faith, frighten me a little. I recognize that unshakable belief, the piety that I grew up with as well. I see it and know it, even as it is not mine anymore.

Her book is a harrowing read. I cannot stop. The massacres, the gruesome indignities, the deaths, the laments of mothers, the terrible, terrible losses. And yet, light, beauty, love, and resistance. Swee Chai's identification with the statelessness of the Palestinians is all the more moving because she refuses to centre her own narrative. After thirty-five years of exile, she is allowed back to inter the ashes of her husband who had fled to London to claim asylum decades prior. Her indomitable clarity of vision, her morality, her tenacity, her persistence—they stay with me. Another way of being, in spite of the state that we grew up in. Her wedding photographs strike me as vaguely familiar, and then I realize that the man standing in front of the young couple is the same priest who baptized me, who married my parents, and my husband and me.

I find a war surgery field manual that she co-authored with two Norwegian doctors. It is a heavy book; the copy I receive is through an interlibrary loan from Queensland University in Australia. It is well-used, its spine barely holding together. I renew it as many times as I can. There are hand-drawn illustrations of wounds, parts of the human body, cross-sectioned to show how to stitch flesh back together again. I learn what it takes to mend bones, save organs (large and small), how to remember that the body simply needs help to heal.

The manual attempts to be comprehensive; it lays out everything from how to start and set up a field hospital to how to manage in the absence of proper supplies. I read exhaustive lists, inventories of medical equipment, instructions on how to sanitize instruments, how to use carpenter's tools when little else is available. How to crack open a rib cage to save the heart.

There is a chapter that is simply titled "Weapons Theory." A title that would not be out of place in the tomes I have been reading that are devoted to promoting the efficacy of the tools of death, of praising their virtues, their oftentimes irreversible damage to limbs, bones, skin, vital organs, eyes, and the rest—too numerous to account for. The surgery manual reminds the reader that it is impossible to treat a wound unless one becomes acquainted with the weapons and munitions that are being used on the battlefield. It describes how local wars have become test sites for new weapons.

Antony Loewenstein writes in his book *The Palestinian Laboratory* that "Palestine is Israel's workshop, where an occupied nation on its doorstep provides millions of subjugated people as a laboratory for the most precise and successful methods of domination." It occurs to me that the war surgery manual knows this instinctively, and articulates it through a different lexicon. The book is dedicated to the surgeons in the war zones of the Third World; the authors note, "we can only admire his strength. His survival proves the effectiveness of his methods."

—

The other books I read detail the history of the weapons industry in Singapore with so much love and care. The pride and patriotism that surrounds these factories of atrocities. It is all abstract violence; there are no test subjects or corpses in these books. Foreword after foreword from celebrated men—politicians, colonels, bureaucrats, all reminiscing. They are nostalgic for those first, heady days of these "pioneer companies," these men with ambition and foresight. One of them notes the thrill and risk of the endeavours: "We're lucky no one got killed."

Another passage from one of the volumes notes, "Using frightfully attractive women dressed in dark blue jumpsuits to demonstrate the weapon, CIS left its mark at every important defence industry exhibition and the arms industry and customers began to take notice." I try but cannot find any pictures of these women. But I imagine they must have looked very much like the famed Singapore Airlines stewardesses in the same era. They have standard-issue lipstick and eyeshadow, regulation hair, faces that are so easy to recognize and yet so hard to remember.

—

Speaking of her desire to first go to Lebanon, Swee Chai tells Francis, "I just can't get any peace not doing anything." This is even as he warns her about the "controversies and politics." She resigns from her post at a UK hospital and arrives in Beirut to find the ruins of a city. She recounts this to her interviewers in her matter-of-fact way:

> You've got blocks and blocks of buildings being bombed to bits. 11-storey building kind of destroyed by implosion bombs and you know that implosion bombs actually suck in isn't it. That's the dual explosive so when it consumes all the oxygen the fireball contracts and sucks everything in. 200 bodies are in it, so I said, they don't need a doctor, you know. So many people have died.

In the middle of Swee Chai's memoir, I find pages and pages of black-and-white photographs. Sabra and Shatila seen through her eyes. These are mostly amateur photographs, a glimpse of what the prose fails to convey. There are the commonplace ruins that have come to define our time, bodies injured or dead, the pained smiles of children and the elderly, an eleven-year-old boy crouching with a grenade launcher, the debris of four hundred shells that hit Shatila in one night. There is a photograph of a young Swee Chai, a petite lady with a heart-shaped face. She is standing in front of a heap of rubble and a burnt-out car. You can see rebar that has worked its way out of its concrete encasing. The caption tells me that the date is September 1982, and that she is looking for survivors. In another photograph, she is operating without a mask, gloves, anaesthetic, or electricity. Her face is a shadowed silhouette against a grey background. Her hair falls between her eye and nose as she bends over the surgery field, her hands illuminated, her delicate fingers poised with a scalpel above an unidentifiable part of a body.

I find a documentary about her online entitled *The Stubborn Doctor*. It was made in England around the same time. Her Singaporean accent is unchanged, a sign of her refusal to assimilate. She speaks of her own helplessness, how she cannot make the killing stop. Later in life, she says, "I should have died many times."

—

In 2024, the Singapore Airshow stoked controversy by hosting numerous Israeli weapons manufacturers and the largest USA partnership pavilion to date. I browse the promotional materials on the Airshow's social media feeds and am struck by one particular video that opens with a beautiful mother and her two little boys. They are all dressed in Singapore air force jumpsuits and standing in front of a fighter jet. Their smiles are wide and innocent, the woman's straight, long hair caught by the wind as if in some commercial. It is an incongruous sight—the domestic and familial in front of a machine designed to kill, at a show intent on showing off more innovative ways to destroy.

There are also the mascots, Captain Leo and Leonette, two anthropomorphized golden-brown lion cubs. Leo has aviator goggles propped over his shaggy mane, while Leonette is coquettish, with a swish of hair covering one eye. She wears a little black miniskirt, while Leo wears only a bomber jacket. I wonder how many strategies were employed to soften the violence inherent in the exhibits.

At the Elbit Systems booth, the company was debuting its newest surveillance drone.

—

In a country that made a large part of its fortune from the arms trade, it seems paradoxical that there are severe laws against being in possession of something as small as a bullet.

In 2018, a labourer working in the ammunition services division of Advanced Material Engineering stole a projectile and flung it into a forested area. This single bullet sparked a two-week search, a sentence of three months in jail, and a $4,000 fine for Goh Wee Eng. A small thing, a 35 mm high-explosive incendiary round, containing 113 Hexotol.

The company hired professional grass-cutters and metal detectors, brought in a police K-9 unit and the army. They worked for almost two thousand man-hours in a desperate search. In the end it was found, buried in the soil, a brief distance from where it had been thrown. In the news coverage of the incident, Deputy

Public Prosecutor Stephanie Koh pointed out that "the accused would have known that all the component parts of the dismantled high-explosive incendiary ammunition rounds were meticulously counted at frequent fixed intervals to ensure that nothing is missing."

Why do we count? What are these tallies for? What is missing? What don't we know?

—

In an interview about her time in Lebanon, Swee Chai describes how a woman tried to give her a baby as the foreign doctors were expelled from the hospital at gunpoint. She takes the baby, which is eventually wrenched from her arms. Another story she keeps returning to in talk after talk, interview after interview, is about the photograph that a group of Palestinian children ask her to take, of them. She recounts, over and over again, what they say to her: "We are the children of Sabra and Shatila. You take a picture and you show it to all your friends, how we are like and we are not afraid."

Dictator

He's a frail man when I finally meet him, as part of the preparations for a televised roundtable involving him and a carefully selected group of young journalists. The words *authoritarian regime* seem flimsy when associated with the liver spots on his face, the wisps of white on his scalp, his slow, stooped gait.

But his beady, combative eyes remain the same ones that we were all accustomed to from posters and television specials. Those eyes unsmiling and calculative even as he planted trees, kissed babies, eulogized late colleagues, and cut ribbons.

As I look at him across the boardroom table, I understand how the nation is obsessed with brief moments of his supposed anguish—so much so that we chronicle the moment of our independence by showing his televised tears on loop.

Later, when his closest allies die, when his wife passes, photographers and cameramen push up against each other, bodies flush against the black, unyielding surfaces of their recording devices, to capture his tears. Is he terrified by his own mortality? The papers print and reprint the image of him supported by his bodyguards as he stiffly tilts down over her coffin to touch her cheek one last time. A husband humanized by loss.

All this has not yet happened when I first encounter him. We have been told to be deferential and quiet. To not complain about the temperature of the room—set at a chilly 18°C to allow his mind to function efficiently despite the tropical heat. My lives, my vitae laid out before him, just one of a series of stacked manila folders. He would not have walked into this meeting without preparation, without his personal assistant who is always a military attaché, interchangeable men who are then put out to pasture in foreign missions or put forward for election as members of Parliament.

My orderly progression through the educational ranks seems to please him; he notes with relish that my credentials have slotted me into the correct position in his hierarchy of things. That I have taken seriously his well-known admonishments to study both in the United States and in China, that I have not broken my bonds or the Official Secrets Act, that I am working assiduously with the national broadcaster to ensure that his government's press releases are transmitted accurately to the general populace, that I have learned to cross my *t*'s and dot my *i*'s and line my eyes with kohl, just so. I am a powdered, rouged, sleekly groomed cog in his giant machine.

It does not really matter what I say to him, small talk or otherwise. There is no possible actual encounter with the man.

Did I really meet him all those years ago? Did I imagine the lights, the cameras, the studio, the earpiece in my ear buzzing with my producer's instructions?

But we are here again at this moment, as he reminds us of what he wants to happen. He is wearing his characteristic navy jacket, collar upturned, his hands clasped in front of him on the table. He smiles at me, shifting the wrinkled skin that covers his cheeks ever so slightly, his eyes unchanging, his small white teeth in neat rows.

"I want this to be a conversation between us. I want you to ask me anything. Ask me anything."

It is at this moment that I realize, more thoroughly than at any other moment, that I have always lived in a dictatorship.

I smile at him, lower my eyelids at his gaze. I feel the contours of power in the room, in its stark lighting, the cold surface of the table, the high-backed chairs. Is there now a kernel of rebellion in me? I imagine how swiftly his security apparatus would incapacitate me if I suddenly pushed back my chair, became a feral animal, and lunged for his delicate old throat.

A decade later, when I learn how to use the blade of my wrist and a small fistful of fabric at a collar to cut off the blood supply to an opponent's brain, I think again of this moment. I have learned more about my body than his. I have learned how I am small but, if I pivot my foot in a particular way, I can exert more than my weight to pin women much larger than me down on the ground, dictate their movements and non-movements.

Can I take him on, then? At that moment, I demur. Later, when the actual interview is being recorded, I allow myself one slip: I ask him about retirement, about a renunciation of power, about unpinning all of us collectively.

He laughs as if I had told a particularly funny joke on air.

He turns his eyes towards me and I know I have found an opening.

"I'll stay as long as I am useful."

—

Because you cannot bear another's weight, because you are so small, you learn alternate moves. You cannot stand as your partner's legs are wrapped around your hips, but you can use the sharpness of those hips to apply a specific pressure on their interlocking ankles.

You place your hands on their pelvic bones, you turn your body in a swift motion. You escape.

Dictation

My eight-year-old self is sitting through a long, arduous session of 听写 tingxie (listening/writing) exercises. The education system insists Mandarin is my mother tongue. I must write out the corresponding character in Sinitic script as my teacher dictates a passage at the front of the classroom.

If I fail to complete this task, as I often do, there will be a red pen jabbed into my arm, my exercise book thrown across the room.

I am resolutely monolingual. I refuse dictation. I do not want to be told what to write and how to write it.

I refuse idiom, idiolect, vocabulary, and thus also national legend, myth, belief.

Later, of course, I realize that this is his language policy. Another way that his control begins with our tongues, our scripts, the only ways in which we can express ourselves. My role as an obedient citizen is circumscribed by the small repeating squares in my exercise book, one for each character. I can never fill each square as it is meant to be filled. Each square should be filled with regular calligraphic strokes, each radical in its own side, each stroke in its set order: upwards, downwards, sideways. Drawing a box, filling it in with minute repetitions, and then sealing it, for good.

—

"Place your knee on the belly and then push down."

You struggle with this instruction, unable to use your weight against another human being. Later, when it is your turn to have your back on the mat, you take a small breath and contract the muscles around your ribs, hardening them against the knee placed just below your sternum, above your navel. Correctly positioned, this can cause discomfort and, occasionally, panic.

—

In a rare moment of weakness, he says that he apologizes for his language policies. That he was wrong to think all of us capable of bilingualism, let alone multilingualism. That our brains were simply not capacious enough to contain many worlds.

But it is not the language itself. In any language, he wanted no dissident poets, education reformers, or guerrilla fighters. He exiled poetry, banned books, and erased lives. But he kept grammar, syntax, Confucian analects, and standardized exams. He did not write each exercise or dictate each test, but it is now impossible for me to think of these moments without feeling the pressure of his decisions on the very way I think my thoughts. His knee on my belly preventing me from speaking, allowing me only to listen and write in an incomprehensible series of strokes.

一

Here's how to escape a knee on your belly: Palm of the hand in the gap between collarbone and throat. Push out. Fold your body at the waist. Move away from your opponent while facing him at all times. It may not work the first time. It never works the first time. Wait. Rest. Catch another opening. Push out again.

Never turn your back to your opponent. If they are well trained, they will immediately hold on to you from behind, putting their legs around your hips and digging their feet into your thighs. If they are fast, they will already have one arm under your neck in a V shape, closing in on your carotid artery.

Like any blood choke, they must know when you are about to lose consciousness. They must stop.

—

Once, on air, my co-host makes an inappropriate political joke. I feel his skin redden beside me as he realizes the magnitude of his gaffe. I remember my own performance, my quizzical turn to the camera, as if trying to cover his out-of-place body with my own. We are so vulnerable in that studio space, the three automated cameras moving up and down their hydraulically powered stands, each a black, glassy eye that reflects our foundation-caked faces. For a moment there he had laid bare the mechanisms of power, who exactly was connected to the money, in this, the most incorruptible of states.

"Do you want to get us all fired? Don't ever do that again!"

The head editor screams from her desk just outside the clear panes of the studio wall. Apologizing profusely, my co-host unbuttons his suit, his skin clammy from the shock of the truth. I hum in wordless sympathy. I open my compact. I powder my nose and check my lipstick.

Spill

Sometimes, petrofictions spill over into reality. They cannot be contained, not really.

In 2024, there is a collision between two ships in the busy lanes of port traffic that ply the Singapore Strait, and four hundred metric tons of oil are released into the sea. This is one in a long line of oil spills off the coast; it is not even the largest one. But perhaps because everything is more visible these days, hundreds of photographs appear on my social media feeds of the black, tarry sludge on the beaches. The complaints about the smell. The hand-wringing annoyance of it all.

And yet no one questions the long history of these incidents or why they happen. It is just a price that must be paid. The workers sent in to clean up the mess are not given the proper protections at first. Only later do we see them in the appropriate hazmat suits. The public relearns the vocabulary of *allision, dispersant, booms, biodegradation, skimmer craft, mitigation*. The authorities run a prediction model, use drone and satellite imagery. If someone encounters an oil-slicked animal, there is a helpline for that.

The last time I saw the sea in Singapore, my father pointed out a long line of container ships and tankers waiting to dock at the port. They blocked the view of the horizon from the tourist beach on the offshore island where we stood. They sat there, motionless in the heat. I wondered about the sailors in these vessels. How long they had gone without seeing their families. How much we see without really seeing.

Scar

We're at a bar, years after my departure. He has come to this city to show his film and we meet to talk about old times. We do this every time we meet—we repeat ourselves, reliving our first encounters with power when we were young journalists. Here now, finally away, we conjure Singapore in our conversations—its weather, its food, its strictures—with precision. I left, but he stayed.

He regales me with his characteristic mordant humour, one way in which we seek to protect ourselves. Speaking of his last film, which was banned, he notes how the timing had been impeccable, they only withdrew his licence the day after—they let him premiere his film and then they banned it. They *made* him premiere his film before banning it. I relive that evening with him: the small talk, the banter, those handshakes, his eyes glazed over with disbelief even with the glare of the camera flashes.

Now, we laugh at his story, feeling the alcohol in our blood, the distance from the dictator. He turns his face towards mine and for a brief moment I freeze. I see another face in his: those hooded eyes, carefully coiffed hair, and thin lips. He is another iteration of the old man—charming, articulate, Cambridge educated. It is only his youth and vigour that have fooled me.

"You still care so much about home. Maybe you should come back."

I laugh off the seductive earnestness in his voice as if it is another joke. The bartender hands me my cocktail and I offer him a taste.

He and I sit at the bar for two, three hours. I know we must seem like lovers, free finally and fully absorbed in each other. But really, what we are doing is simply allowing ourselves to exist in the small space that we have made between us, one where we are free to laugh at the contradictions and foibles that a dictatorship produces. We exchange stories of unreasonable bureaucrats, careerist politicians, and simpering subordinates. We share our outrage at the arrest of public intellectuals, show trials, and long exiles. We let ourselves imagine what would happen if he died. And see in ourselves thousands, millions of us, moulded in his image, enabling the machinery to crank on.

I drink more than I intend to. He only has his one beer. We eat what passes for Spanish tapas in this northern city: cubed and fried potatoes, deeply salty canned anchovies, blood sausage on small slices of toast. The bar smells of the sea, of other coastlines and other evenings.

"What if he died? What would change?"

"Nothing, I suppose. Everything is already in place."

—

We pause to say goodbye outside the bar. The long summer shadows and golden twilight cast a sheen on the passing cars and sidewalks. I slip my bicycle helmet on before he envelops me in his customary embrace.

Soon he will be on a plane going back. He will make this trip over and over again, flying over oceans and land masses to screen and re-screen his films. He will win prizes, especially for the works that are banned back home.

"Always a pleasure."

He intones these words in his unplaceable accent. I feel the chill again. That muscle memory reaching across the years and continents. He says my name, not just my name but its shortened form, conveying an intimacy and history that makes me turn away quickly. I fish my bicycle keys from my bag; their reassuring weight slides into the heavy lock around the frame. A twist of the wrist and the lock falls from the post. I turn to look at him one last time. He is already walking down the street, his blue linen suit catching the dusk light. Grasping my handlebars, I mount my bicycle and slip into the busy street.

—

On one of my visits back to Singapore, we agree to meet again. We walk in the dark, humid night, illuminated by orange street lights and the fluorescent tubes so common in these public housing estates, ones that confuse your circadian rhythms and tell you that it is daytime all the time. We take the staircase down to the car park. I have not ridden pillion since the one and only time I was in another country for a work assignment. There, it was unnerving to sit so close to a stranger whose love for speed and velocity would take me to a gracious restaurant in a courtyard.

But here we are now, in front of his scooter, and he takes out an extra helmet that he has brought for the occasion. I think about who else has worn this helmet and who else might wear it after. As I think of what he might say if someone found one of my long hairs coiled inside the darkness of its insides, he hands me what looks like an awkwardly small skullcap.

"It's clean. I just washed it."

I push my hair over one shoulder and hand him my heavy bag of books as I try to adjust the cap on my head. He places my belongings in the top box and then reaches back to help me adjust the liner. I clamber awkwardly behind him, the material of my dress bunching up in the front. I'm not sure where to put my hands, so they end up clenched over the handlebars just under my seat.

I'm nervous just from him carefully negotiating the exit from the parking garage. Each slight movement to the right and to the left means adjusting my weight to the minute manoeuvres he is making. We pull alongside the parking barrier, wait for the sensor to read his card so we can finally leave. I consider my position just behind him, my feet resting on the footrests elevated just behind his legs. If I lean too much into him, our helmets collide.

We ride down the roads that I have always known. This must be strange for you, he turns to say. The ordinary routes that I have driven on, taken buses on, been driven on, sometimes perhaps even walked. But this is different. The wind is in my hair, I can barely hear what is being said. The cars are close, so close to us. We speed down this highway, although I can tell he isn't going even half as fast as he usually does. My body is tense, hands gripping the handles; my back aches from anticipating the starts and stops.

—

I'm trying to remember the look on his face when he first came up to me all those years ago. Puzzlement, fear, bewilderment. We had just run headlong into a wall of power and unknown machinations. He asked me whether it was real. To check the recording of what had just transpired—forgetting that editing would render any recorded proof pointless in any case. We were in a dusty backroom, full of old props and remnants of other spectacles. The backroom of propaganda. What would later be televised would be a pastel echo of what had happened, another carefully managed conversation with the constituents, the youth—the ongoing, ever-unfinished consolidation of control.

So it seems inevitable that we are drawn together again and again by this formative experience. Like survivors of some wreck, pulled down by unknown monsters. What is the distance between what is desired and what is possible? I came up to its face, came so close to it I could listen to its breath, touch the air around its skin, change the texture of the space it lived in.

In retrospect, is all desire then false? Or is it a mere accounting? To see the other, to see oneself as more than a blunt instrument, a cog, a moving part now twisted ever so slightly out of shape. Parts of this machine must endure moments of great stress so as to ensure the lubricated running of the larger whole. I see him and the small dictatorships that he is drawn to, that he facilitates. I see our attempts to wrest control over these narratives, all narratives, to avoid mediocrity and repetition, always wondering if others will truly see you.

I look into those small, hooded eyes, I try to locate the venom, the sting. I try to understand the irresistible draw. Desire that never leaves us, a constant low hum of it during the day no matter how many thousands of miles separate us. The unheard frequencies of our bodies aging slowly.

Throat

The man clears his throat. He sits, perched on the edge of his chair, and begins to read to the audience. The words mark the air around his body. They speak of other bodies, different, apart from factory lines, gross domestic products, happiness. They adorn the air with images of lips, shoulders, hips, thighs, glances, and skin. These words do not belong to our regulated desires, to population targets or the sparsely decorated rooms—a potted palm, a tasteful landscape—where we join our lives, two by two, signatures affixed to the official documentation.

The audience shifts uncomfortably in their seats. In our state, there is none but sanctioned desire, the kind that leads to pink-walled labour suites and laminated certificates of live births. The quick, painless clamp on an umbilical cord, its pulsations turning grey. The indignity of floral arrangements festooned with silver balloons and stuffed animals. The garments of newborns fastened into their cardboard-and-plastic packaging with small, sharp pins.

The man continues. His words mark the space around us. He lifts them from the page as if they were birds taking flight.

This moment does not linger, it is brief and contained. The man continues to read the memory of two men, pressed up against each other under the blue light of a dance club. They kiss, lips on each other's mouths and throats, oblivious to the bodies around them. I fear for them. Their bodies are so vulnerable in the half-light, the dusk of this moment. I suppress my desire to place myself between the poet and the rest of the crowd, to make him invisible. The men I have come with laugh this impulse off. Scoffing at my size, my seemingly misplaced fear.

As the years pass, many of these same men, their desires carefully regulated and sometimes even submerged, will rise in the ranks of the system. I know them by their attention to the minutiae of their lives, order, control. Their careful concealments spilling over to all aspects of their lives and bodies. A tie neatly knotted, a shirt immaculately pressed, a muscle worked on repeatedly, manila folders on a desk meticulously stacked. A perfect alignment. There is no other choice if one is ambitious. No use risking exposure or denouncement. Sometimes, one of them places a hand on the small of my back, as if trying out a new habit. I let that hand stay there for as long as it takes for him to understand what it is he really wants. I am patient.

Gap

In August 2022, I have two seizures. Grand mal, they call it. The great illness.

I remember so little of the days and weeks that followed. I am told that my seizure was a shocking, unprecedented, and traumatic event for my family. That my husband repeatedly called out my name, tried to wake me, held me, and prevented me from hitting my head on the floor. He tried to pry my jaws open to prevent me from hurting myself. My older son thought I was dying when I turned blue from apnea. My younger son, ever the calm one, called 911 and asked for instructions on what to do for me.

My neighbours later tell me that they heard the ambulance come barrelling down the crescent, two paramedics coming into our house. They saw me later, being carted out of the house in a seated stretcher. I am told I was pale as a sheet.

—

The last thing I remembered was an intense feeling of dizziness, nausea, a hazy and overwhelming loss of control and consciousness.

A doctor grasping both of my arms and asking me to pull as hard as I can. A bright light shining into my eyes, one at a time. My husband's voice and his raspy beard as he kissed me goodbye. A nurse helping me stagger to use the washroom. Another who gave me a small container of yogurt and a pack of biscuits. These were the best things I had ever eaten in my life. I had overlooked my hunger.

In the weeks that follow, I treat myself as a fragile and unpredictable creature. I religiously take the hexagonal pink pills that are supposed to keep my seizures at bay. They make my skin erupt in hives when it is exposed to the cold. I discover this unwittingly when my bare legs, clad in summer shorts, encounter the freezer section in the supermarket. Large welts that are unbearably itchy erupt immediately on my thighs. I stand in line to pay, trying not to scratch, trying not to bring attention to myself. Have I become allergic to this country, this province, this life?

How little we can control of our bodies, really. All those routines, exercises that we practise, correcting the smallest of details, the exactitude of angles, how our bodies are placed. How it can go all awry with the smallest misfiring of neurons, chemicals, and cells. The microscopic betrays us. A mutation, a fault, an evolution—or a revolt.

"I'm alive but in which
organ did my body
store my disrepair?"

—JASON WEE, *IN SHORT, FUTURE NOW*

How have I held this in my body all this while?

How long has it been there?

Where did it come from?

Dictum

Twice a year I am tested on my diction, as if they know that my accent is not a fixed creature. We are led into a soundproof booth where two or three veterans wait for us with clipboards and checklists. We are given a list of words—names of obscure Thai politicians, French tennis stars, Argentinian footballers, local roads. We are made to repeat each one slowly into a condenser microphone. When we are done, the assessors patiently repeat our errors back to us, giving us advice about where to place our tongue on our teeth, our palate, and our lips in order to make the correct sounds in the correct order.

We learn how to speak all over again. For it is a slippery thing, an accent, and I have spent a long time cultivating its slipperiness in order to adapt, to assimilate, and to escape. Vowels and consonants travel from the back of my throat to the hum of my mouth depending on who I am speaking to, who speaks to me. The timbre of my voice changes depending on the inflections of the situation.

—

Is speaking freely and slipping between languages and accents akin to being free? Now you consider this as your opponents wrap their calves above your hips, their muscles pulling you into their guard. When you wrestle control of their hands, some other language is conceived. How are the words pronounced?

You fail many times. You fall on your partners as they embrace you laughing, catching your clumsiness and encouraging you to try again. Their accents: Peruvian, Danish, Québécois, Jamaican, Somali. This is not poise, posture, diction, or dictation. In the change room, you try to talk about your past. But you are unable to find the right words, in the right language, the correct order of phrases.

—

In my classroom now, I speak with a different voice, a changed accent.

In quiet moments, I find the muscles of my face and around my spine arranged in their familiar configurations, my neck held back to the right degree for my eyes to meet the camera.

Once, during a course evaluation by an older white male colleague whose stentorian voice commands the room with no effort at all, I am told that I have a verbal tic. I keep repeating the word *right*. I use the syllable as a question, a pleading, a filler, a stopgap measure. I am told to get rid of it since it annoys.

Since then, I pause at the end of my sentences, feel the desire to test the room, meet the eyes of my students, venture for a consensus of sorts. I feel the muscles of my mouth reach for the memory of my first voice, that tone and that accent. The taste of it on my tongue.

Right?

Video

I slip a tape out of my handbag and slot it into the large, ungainly machine. The high-pitched whir of footage going in reverse fills my headphones until, in the fuzz of the screen, I can see the frame I am looking for.

The machine has sensitive controls that allow me to toggle each frame in and out of my vision. I can halt someone mid-syllable, catch a person in the act, each minute gesture a freeze-frame on my screen.

The video editors who have been manipulating the machines every day for years on end know their quiet quirks and invisible preferences. They flick the controls with their wrists and fingers, slamming down rapidly on buttons to pause, splice, and overlay. We flirt with the nicest of them, buy them treats from the canteen or from our trips abroad so that they will spare a quick moment for us, work their magic to turn twenty-two minutes of unremarkable footage into a snappy one minute and thirty seconds of carefully packaged soundbites and newsreel.

I do not usually spend much time considering the packages of reality that I am creating.

I forget that I can make time slow down to a crawl, make it speed up into a blur.

—

Sitting in a darkened screening room, I watch Tan Pin Pin's *To Singapore, with Love,* a film that the state has banned. Every single scene save one has been filmed outside its borders. I watch:

A man frying a wok of noodles.

A woman speaking and crying.

A man reciting a poem.

A child playing in a backyard in England.

A man retrieving the battered suitcases he brought with him the night he escaped.

A group of people listening to a eulogy.

A man singing.

I think about all the ordinary things that have been made illegal. All the things that we should not or cannot do, or film, or think, or talk about.

The white Canadian projectionist who is assisting me in testing the reel looks at me quizzically.

"How can this be banned? There doesn't seem to be anything offensive about it."

I try again to explain where power begins and how it presses down on us. But it doesn't come out quite right. There are no words to explain what calibration feels like. How we do not know where a boundary is until we run into it, full-bodied, smashing ourselves headlong into an invisible barrier. Drawing back, only to find ourselves with a bloodied lip, a cracked rib, a broken heart.

—

The video on the computer screen is small and blurry. I am watching a clip of the police raiding the office of an old activist in Singapore. She knows the routine, having been swept up in the 1980s during a notorious police operation that accused men and women campaigning for workers' rights of being Marxists. I don't know why they have chosen her.

I can just make out a group of men and women, standing over a messy office desk with an elderly woman seated before them. The man who is wearing an official lanyard and identification speaks in even tones, as if to a child. He is explaining why he is taking the woman's computer away, why they will take it apart and, perhaps, put it together again. He shows her the seal they have placed on the seams of the machine in order to prove that no one will tamper with it until they open it up, exposing its circuitry and wiring, extracting the necessary proof of the woman's guilt as well as the invisible connections she has made with all the others who resist the state.

The woman protests, her voice breaking with her barely contained rage and fear.

The man continues to speak in low, hushed tones, his accent smoothed over for the occasion. Placating, lulling, excusing.

The woman does not make a move to rise as the other people in the room continue to move around her study, shuffling papers, opening boxes, rummaging like scavengers looking for a morsel.

The video cuts out, but it stays with me. It does not leave my body.

—

On another trip back to the island, I sit in a darkened theatre watching Jason Soo's documentary *1987: Untracing the Conspiracy*. It is a quiet film of testimonials, stories of late-night arrests, long detentions, forced confessions. I am in one of the few independent film theatres in Singapore, housed in an older high-rise that always seems to be under threat of demolition.

The others in the audience seem nervous, unsure of their place in their seats, looking around surreptitiously in case someone is recording their reactions, their expressions, their minute movements. I wonder why they bothered to purchase the tickets to this screening. They must have known the risks in our small state. Perhaps their curiosity got the better of them. Perhaps they had to know. Perhaps they had to hear it for themselves. I turn to the acquaintance next to me and, in the dim shadows, I make note of the swollen cartilage of his ear. I recognize the calloused joints on his hand. I know we will later speak the same language of takedown, joint-lock, blood choke.

I turn back to the screen and listen to accounts of sleep deprivation, temperature control, psychological intimidation. The interview subjects are filmed in a light-filled room, their sun-aged faces and wrinkles around their eyes turned to the camera lens. The film cuts back and forth, from them to archival footage to carefully saved photographs, then ends abruptly—a work half-made, perhaps always doomed to incompletion.

I know that there are other, more profound tragedies than this one. But if we do not listen to these stories, how can we be patient with other atrocities? If we turn away from our own histories of repression, then how can we feel empathy for the victims of other despots?

When the lights return, a small man shuffles into the front of the room with the filmmaker. He is an activist whose confession was coerced on national television a quarter of a century ago. There were clues, his friends noted, through which he tried to signal that something was not right. For one, his hair was parted to the wrong side, in what seemed to be a deliberate message to those who knew him. We lived in a state where the significance of the smallest of dissident gestures seemed to be magnified a thousandfold.

Immediately, as the man approaches the front of the room, a third of the audience begins to get to their feet. It is one thing to see and hear these stories onscreen. It is another to witness the wreckage of that moment in living flesh. To be in the same room, breathing the same air, smelling the same forgotten yet omnipresent fear. Theirs is an unspoken, collective desire: a removal from this scene. A decontamination. They push against the knees of the seated people, a quiet desperation to exit as rapidly as possible. They seek to leave before the man begins to speak. They avoid making eye contact with those of us who choose to stay and listen. We are not a collective.

We are not an assembly. We are not even witnesses. Perhaps his words will capture them, as birds in a net. Except their wings have already been clipped.

—

I watch another film, Boo Junfeng's *The Apprentice*, a subtle critique of the use of the death penalty in Singapore. This time it is the aural details that wrench my heart.

The bird calls of my childhood. The repeated sounds of opening and closing gates. The high-pitched hum of a commuter bus route.

How do you record the sound of oppression? The sounds of an efficient machine, made up of other human beings, who, even when faced with the task of murdering another human being, take it on with levity and pragmatism? Later, I find out that many of the scenes of incarceration and state punishment were filmed on a continent five hours away from the island. The filmmaker having judged it too controversial even to try to obtain permission from the relevant authorities.

How did he re-create that light, those sounds, that sense of the early morning execution in a wholly familiar space and time?

—

Once, a famous film director comes on the set of the newsroom to do an interview for his new piece of filmic allegory. He's made it so lush, so melodramatic, and so Gothic that the censors would rather not read into it and have let it pass without cuts. After all, no one would believe that this tale laden with sex, spectacle, and haunting could possibly be anything but a work of fiction. Another way in which we evade the weight of power, its ability to excise, amputate, destroy, make incoherent, impose a way of seeing onto our private visions. But if those visions are Technicolored, absurdist, full of scheming siblings and ritual and spectacle, perhaps just by watching it we can quietly laugh, a sort of small, private laugh that only occurs deep in one's throat and chest, that no one else can hear. Is it illegal, too, to laugh? Who can really explain what that laughter is for? Is it of amusement, surreality, or some deep and abiding pain?

The director turns to me as I am ushering him out of the television studio. He asks for my story, and I tell him that my time here is almost done—my years of work to repay a scholarship at a university abroad. He says, "I look forward to seeing what you will do next."

These words stay with me; they haunt me in ways greater than whatever he intended with the small phrase of encouragement. What was next? How did he know it would matter? And of course all he meant was a future apart from the weight of this obligation pressing down on me, away from the strictures of how I bore my body, measured my words, refused to look power in the eye, having been slighted and beaten down in so many small ways.

How I would, in effect, be learning how to speak again, without constraints, or fear of reprisal, or lack of an audience.

How they would be my words, and not someone else's, carefully scripted to please and to placate, emerging from my mouth, each vowel and consonant crisp and so carefully formed, as if truth were as simple as received pronunciation.

If I learned to speak my own words, to write them down, with no fear. That I would, in fact, be learning how to live.

Falling

Each trip home has been to bear witness to my mother's further deterioration: her inability to bring spoonfuls of food to her mouth; a regression to merely using fingers to eat; finally, only the tiniest portions on a spoon to her lips, the caregiver willing her not to choke. *Dysphagia* is such a horrible word. Difficulty or discomfort in swallowing, as a symptom of disease. *Phagia*, Greek for "to eat," a function so basic we don't even think about it as we chew and swallow. Now all her meals are puréed beyond recognition. Texture is such a large part of the pleasure in eating. Even her drinking water must be thickened by the addition of starch.

At first, I was able to lift her from wheelchair to bed, from bathroom floor to standing, from car to wheelchair and back again. Now there is a deadening of weight, her body unable to help me as I bear it.

"J, I can't express my feelings to you."

Are there feelings about me? Are there feelings that cannot be shared with me? Those are not the same things. My mother has never been the most demonstrative of mothers. I fear the same of myself, so I remember to offer kisses and ask my sons for hugs.

The only moments I have left with my father are when she is secured—in bed, in a wheelchair, in the front passenger seat of the car. Where we have snatches of conversation, of what is and what is to come.

—

It's good you had two sons, my grandmother says. Not like your mother, who only had one daughter. And you're so far away, we only see you every once in a while. It's as if she didn't have any children at all.

Link

This is what an earpiece feels like: It's an extension of yourself, the way you are plugged into the hub of screens, levers, and buttons in the studio. The way you are connected to the banter, the invective, the instructions that are spoken into the microphone in that enclosed control room. The constant link to the power behind the scene that you see. You learn to recognize the different voices in the foreground and background. That intimacy of another's speech in your ear.

We are made up with the same palettes and powders, hair primped and disciplined by the same implements, our molecules mingling in the dusty backrooms. We might wear the same blazers, the scent of another never quite dissipating, even with dry cleaning. But the earpieces: Each one of us is assigned our own; there is no sharing of these attachments.

When these buildings are abandoned and demolished, when these links are cut and gone, as is their fate—what will it be to lose this patina? To lose these connections, these accumulations, the sediment and strata of skin cells, hair, arguments, compliances, quiet trysts, echoes of laughter and tears.

Such human parts of the grand machine.

Years later, I parse the final photographs of these edifices. Their rooms, corridors, staircases, vacant. These were dream-making factories, where we manufactured pleasure, danger, love, and also authority and truth. I remember the banal physicality of it. Those hot afternoons, the cold of the air conditioning turned up to preserve the machines, that light-filled cafeteria with soaring ceilings and good food. Now all rubble and emptiness. The land considered more valuable than its close-guarded memories.

Imaging

They tell me that I have a lesion in my brain. No way right now, with the limited vision of the magnetic resonance imaging, to tell what it really is. Or is not. These are just shadows and light. The radiologists who read them are fortune tellers and prophets. They see in the darkness and flare all that we cannot.

Glioma, tumefactive demyelinating lesion. The diagnosis is impossible to glean from these phantoms.

I will be sent for four, five, six more tests, perhaps just the beginning of many more. How many ways can one see the body? Or not be seen at all. Mine will be stripped, laid bare, sliced in three dimensions by doses of radiation and intense magnetic forces. They will ask me if I have metal in my eyes, in my abdomen, on the clasps and fixings of my clothes.

Lungs, spleen, liver, kidneys, stomach, intestines, ovaries, uterus, and all the spaces in between. A hunt, a diagnosis of exclusion.

The lesion is not where they expected it to be.

The lesion is larger than they expected it to be.

The lesion is an incidental finding.

I imagine that this peanut-sized abnormality, damage, is my grief. I am not where I expected to be.

—

"The last time I looked at an MRI of a brain was when my mother was diagnosed with progressive supranuclear palsy."

I say this offhandedly to the resident doctor at the multiple sclerosis clinic.

"That must have been terrible," she replies. "So much atrophy."

In my mind, I superimpose my mother's scan with

my own. Numerous doctors tell me that the two conditions have nothing to do with each other. They are not connected. We are no longer connected, she and I. Trying to trace lines linking our bodies is impossible. We fail.

Unbidden, a memory of her pursed-lipped smile comes to me. The one she used as she tried on something new or put on an outfit and some lipstick. A private moment. Perhaps I am now the only person who remembers this small gesture. She is already ash; I remind myself of this again and again. An urn of ash placed and sealed into a niche. I will not see her again.

—

I have lost count of the number of times I have lain down in the sarcophagus-like MRI machine. I have been to all three in this small city. This time, a pair of goggles is placed on my face and questions, words, photographs, equations flash before my eyes in two-second intervals.

"It doesn't matter if you get the answers right," says the doctor, "what matters is that you try. The blood will flow to the parts of your cortex that are activated, and they will light up on the screen."

She has a half sleeve of tattoos on her right arm and when I tell her I love the peonies, she points out the line of hieroglyphics subtly placed within the flowers.

"It means 'brain.'"

—

Lately, because of the anti-seizure medication, I have been having vivid, unforgettable dreams. In these dreams, every place that is beloved to me is laid over the other. Turn a corner and you are in a medieval Italian town, another bend and you are on a beach on the Pacific coast, yet another and you are in a city in the tropics. I am in New York walk-ups, Thai eating houses, classrooms in New England, streets in Hong Kong.

I think of all the places I have been and still want to go to. I wonder whether I will ever take a long-haul flight again. Like my mother's, my world has suddenly shrunk into the companionable presence of my dogs, the predictability of our walks, and the video screens that open up into the faces of my dearest and oldest friends. The interruptions and stutters of the digital connections now inescapable parts of our conversations.

I become so familiar with the waiting rooms of various hospitals and clinics in this small prairie city. I banter with the nurses and become accustomed to the lines they start in my veins, filling them with contrast, the dye that will make my vessels light up.

In one waiting room, there is a large wall covering that details the history of magnetic resonance imaging in Saskatchewan. As I read, I learn that the potash mining company Nutrien was the lead donor in a campaign to raise funds for the first MRI scanner in the province, in 1990. That this is how the PET-CT Centre at the Royal University Hospital came to be named after the company.

I do more research on the province I have lived in for all these years: all that potash, formed from the evaporation of an inland sea hundreds of millions of years ago. A geological age. How I had mistaken this land, with its dryness and distance from the ocean. All around me were the remains of a dissolved sea, its ashes in a layer of salts—the 280-kilometre-long band of the Prairie Evaporite Formation. Potash from Saskatchewan spread out over its fields, the fields of other provinces, countries, continents. In our veins and bodies as well.

—

I make my husband count the number of staples on my scalp.

Twenty-two, he says.

I tell a joke about them that I cannot now remember.

A sample of my brain is sent to the provincial laboratory in Saskatchewan, and then eventually to Toronto.

A part of me is gone.

A hamartoma.

"[H]aphazard normal tissue growth and architectural patterns of cytologically normal cells native to the local site."

A part of me that is faulty.

"Hamartomas cause morbidity by various mechanisms such as infection, infarction, pressure/obstruction, hemorrhage/anemia, fracture, and neoplastic transformation . . .

". . . a developmental error . . .

". . . disordered replications of normal tissue cells. The underlying mechanisms of anomalous replications are not fully recognized."

Ash

Since my mother's death, I have not been able to work. But I have been doing.

The doing has, in fact, been frenzied: visiting banks with their cold rooms and sharply dressed bankers; sitting with nervous men who are surrounded by a collection of sample urns; flipping through plasticized pages offering various religiously appropriate "themes" and decor; receiving guests who say the same thing over and over again.

Talking, talking, talking, sorting, packing.

"You fall apart later," an older friend says.

I've cooked, cleaned, washed, and eaten. The necessities. I've taken planes, driven cars, swum in lakes, gone for long walks.

Things fall apart, come undone, papers accumulate, messages go unanswered; the pile of books, unread, grows ever taller.

I did read, I have read, I read even on that last sleepless night, listening to her laboured breathing in the intensive care unit. The nurse remarking, "She's not really here with us."

—

I sort through my mother's collection of unworn scarves: silk, batik, cotton, paisley, floral. I wear each one in turn, more than one in a day sometimes. The smell of the old, humid, dusty cupboard. There are ungiven gifts that she bought during her travels, squirrelled away for some child or visitor or occasion. Jewellery and bags that were never used.

I divide her clothes between her caregivers and myself. They urge me to try on and take more things. But I cannot. They spent so much more time with her than I did, towards the end. Are these clothes, some tailored to fit my mother exactly, sufficient compensation? I know what it is to have cared for her, even as it became too much for me.

I remember lying next to her, unable to sleep for worry and vigilance. I remember helping her use the toilet in the early hours of the morning, struggling under her weight.

There are many ways to die.

—

When I say I miss my mother, what I mean is that I miss her before her illness, though the memory of that person fades every day. This is not to say I stopped loving my mother when she was ill. I loved her even more through her frailty. But this is to say, she stopped being my mother.

For me, the only way through caregiving was detachment. I subsumed myself in it. I was patient, chipper, attentive, watchful, and never too tired.

But I was abandoned. I bear no anger towards her or even the disease. This is simply a fact. It was not even anticipatory grief. There was no time for that. No time to pause and imagine what this might mean.

—

My father notes that my mother had two deaths: one a cardiac arrest in a park, and another after her revival, when she knew for sure that I had returned to be by her side.

I watched on the machines as her heart rate plummeted. I cupped her face in my hands.

"I'm here, Mum. You can go now. It's okay."

—

When I arrived for the last time, my mother's face was changed. For years, I had seen anguish, strain, expressionlessness, pain, and joy. Sometimes a hopelessness, a resignation, an apologetic smile. Towards the end, her illness often made it impossible to tell what she was thinking. Her laugh and frown lines began to smooth out without use. Their disappearance made her seem younger than she was, concurrent with her failing ability to care for herself.

But this was different—a deep relaxation that was unnaturally calm. A rest that had eluded her for a decade or more. A sharp contrast to the insomnia that first predicted the start of this ordeal. So here now, even amidst the tubes and wires, she seemed finally at peace. The muscles of her face completely lax, in a deep slumber from which she could not or would not wake.

—

We collect her ashes, which are really bone fragments, femur bone to pieces of skull, patterns swirled by heat into their concavities. The undertaker tells me that the large parts of the cranium have to be placed in the urn last.

I am reminded of the Singaporean-Australian poet Boey Kim Cheng's elegy "After the Fire." Our actions echo his, across years. This anonymous room, site of so many tears and mourners gingerly placing each bone into an urn:

He starts from the base
an anatomy lesson in Hokkien
showing us what we didn't see
in life, where it went wrong, the rot.

My father continues to speak to these remains as they are moved from funeral parlour to waiting room in the columbarium, before being slotted into their appointed niche. Sealed off from whatever fate awaits the rest of us.

Tide

What do we inherit? What have I inherited? A clenched hand, wrist turned down, fingers curled as if in pain or focus. I find my own hands in this state, every now and then, unconscious. I see my mother on a video call, showing me that she can still open up her hand, holding a palm to the screen.

My favourite photograph of her is one where she is on the roof of the Duomo in Milan. I had the pretensions of using black-and-white film in my early twenties. I capture her with her head turned to the side, looking off at the view. She is framed by the Gothic spires and her face is calm, maybe happy.

—

I wonder what gestures my sons will inherit from me. What fears, tastes, dislikes. Already they avoid my writing, caution me against the literary, the poetic. They know, already, the power and insufficiency of words, the awkwardness of waves of emotion and sentiment. They mimic my accent sometimes with affection. But they will never truly carry that cadence, the one into which my mouth and throat relax.

My older son was in utero as I dashed from news van to the editing studio to the transmission room. Did that stress course through his blood as it did mine? What did my younger one discern from the voices around him? What did he hear as I read the news of the day, as I carried him everywhere with me?

I remember their sticky toddler cheeks and necks in the tropical heat, their sandy feet washing off in the bath. I place a photograph of them with my mother close to my front door, now. I believe, perhaps falsely, that neither of them will ever be able to live where I grew up. They would be misplaced, like me.

I do not wish them my anxiety, or the mutations in my genes that have led me here. I learned how to eschew the standards that I was held to, the ambitions and paths I was taught to desire. Did I not take them away fast enough? Even as it was to another country whose name seemed like freedom but which was, simply, ultimately, another part of Empire.

So much is unknown, unknowable. There were orphans on both sides of my family. What were their families like, moving across the waters to settle? No one will be able to tell us. They are not in any archive that we can find or restore.

I want to stave off this inheritance, their inheritance. I push myself to the limits of my physical endurance at times. My body obeys and disobeys. I wonder how to escape this endless, relentless tide of decline.

What is there left to lose?

Acknowledgements

To my editors, Hilary Lo and Dionne Brand. Thank you for your generosity and inspiration, for letting this book be its own thing, and for helping me see my writing in a much larger context.

To everyone at Alchemy, especially to Lynn Henry and all those involved in the publication process. I am so honoured to be part of your path-breaking work.

To the editors of *Catapult Magazine*, *Brick: A Literary Journal*, *Ex-Puritan*, and *Evergreen Review* for allowing my writing to find its audience. Thanks as well to Jackie Kaiser, who took the time to speak to a complete stranger.

To those who read earlier drafts of this work: Katherine Magyarody, Rawi Hage, Madeleine Thien, Laurie S. Graham, David Chariandy, Adie Todd, Adrian De Leon, Jean L'Hour, and my fiction seminar at the University of Toronto where the initial pieces of this book were written. To Catherine Imbriglio, for my first-ever creative non-fiction workshop at Brown University.

To friends, scholars, artists, filmmakers, and writers whose insights have contributed to this text. Thank you to Tan Pin Pin, ila, Jeremy Tiang, Jason Wee, Nazry Bahrawi, Faris Joraimi, E.K. Tan, Mayee Wong, Shaoling Ma, Girish Daswani, Nadine Chan, Chan Cheow Thia, Sheela Jane Menon, Brian Bernards, Kalyanee Mam, Juria Toramae, Robert Zhao, Charles Lim, Hong Lysa, Sai Siew Min, Sim Chi Yin, Souvankham Thammavongsa, Wayde Compton, Lucy Davis, Cecily Nicholson, Jerrine Tan, Lydia Kwa, Tania De Rozario, Cheryl Naruse, Weihsin Gui, and Alfian Sa'at. There are so many more of you and I hope you know who you are.

To the activists and activist-scholars in Singapore. I have been inspired by my fellow AcademiaSG editors and alumni Teo You Yenn, Cherian George, Linda Lim, Corrie Tan, and Ian Chong; and all the folks working to make the city more humane, just, and equitable—Bani Haykal, Stephanie Chok, Kirsten Han, and others. In questioning the status quo and its absurdities, yours is the hardest work of all.

To my journalist and news production colleagues in Singapore. The first seeds of this book were planted during my time as a reporter and producer-presenter in Singapore. While I will always be ambivalent about that period in my life, I owe a great deal to you and the ways in which you provided camaraderie and support. Your professionalism and dedication (despite all the restrictions under which we were working) are to be lauded.

To my instructors and partners on the jiu-jitsu and kick-boxing mats in Toronto and Saskatoon. You gave me the gift of epiphanic moments that created this text. Thank you for being patient and gentle with this forever white belt.

To my colleagues at the University of Saskatchewan and Simon Fraser University for valuing my practice as a creative writer alongside my career as an academic.

To the neurology team and nurses at the Royal University Hospital in Saskatoon. I placed everything that made me myself in your hands and have so much gratitude for your care.

To my chosen family in Canada. You have made it possible for me and my loves to thrive in the diaspora. Much love to Cindy, Lisa P, Phoebe, Amanda, Kathleen, Katherine, Nadine, Phanuel, Thy, Kylee-Anne, CJ, Nikko, Karina, Olga, Tenille, Lisa V, David, Jean, Pete, Rupaleem, Marc, Sean, and the late Don and Y-Dang. Thanks to everyone who opened their homes to us, nourished us, and helped us through some of the hardest times in our life.

To my oldest friends: Sze, Usha, Laurel, Ernie, Marlene, Alexis, Wendy, Marilyne, Colette, and Gigi, who have always made us feel at home wherever we happen to find ourselves.

To my family in Italy and Singapore, for the decades of love, comfort, and understanding.

To Kyin Thay and Win, for doing the work of caregiving for my mother and grandmother for so many years in the most intimate and difficult ways.

To my father, who has shown me over and over again what unconditional love means.

To my sons Luca and Dante—you carry so much of me in you but are so much more than I can conceive. Thank you for putting up with the excesses of your overly political and poetic mother.

To my partner Giuliano in life, music, hilarity, love, sickness, and health.

And finally, to the memory of my mother. So much of her humour, spark, and vigour was robbed from us in the last decade of her life. But she persisted, and continues to be in my heart and thoughts, always.

Works Cited and Consulted

Alberta Government. "Alberta's Oil Production and Where It Goes." https://open.alberta.ca/dataset/b8fea8da-848f-4d04-be0f-983787f88694/resource/10be9c86-9b98-43e5-b16a-904b95800612/download/11-albertas-oil-production-and-where-it-goes-formated.pdf.

Ali, Syed A., and Francesk Mulita. "Hamartoma." *National Library of Medicine*, March 14, 2023. www.ncbi.nlm.nih.gov/books/NBK562298/.

Ang, Swee Chai. *From Beirut to Jerusalem: 40th Anniversary Edition*. Islamic Book Trust, 2019.

Ang, Swee Chai. "Swee Chai Ang: Orthopaedic Surgeon, Aid Worker, Activist & Author." Interview by Kash Akhtar and Peter Bates. *See one / do one*, podcast, Orthohub, February 2, 2022. https://orthohub.xyz/swee-chai-ang-orthopaedic-surgeon-aid-worker-activist-author/.

Bal, Charan. "Dealing with Deportability: Deportation Laws and the Political Personhood of Temporary Migrant Workers in Singapore." *Asian Journal of Law and Society* 2, no. 2 (2015): 267-284.

Boey, Kim Cheng. "After the Fire." From *After the Fire: New and Selected Poems*. Firstfruits Publications, 2006.

Boo, Junfeng, dir. *Apprentice*. Singapore: Akanga Film Productions et al., 2016.

Burr, Christina. "Some Adventures of the Boys: Enniskillen Township's 'Foreign Drillers,' Imperialism, and Colonial Discourse, 1873-1923." *Labour/Le Travailleur* 51 (2003): 47–80.

Cameron, Paul, dir. *Westworld: The New World*. Season 3, episode 4, "The Mother of Exiles." Aired April 5, 2020, on HBO.

Chan, C.K. "Eugenics on the Rise: A Report from Singapore." *International Journal of Health Services* 15, no. 4 (1985): 707-712.

Chew, Valerie. "Laju hijacking." *Singapore Infopedia*, 2008. https://www.nlb.gov.sg/main/article-detail?cmsuuid=54700656-62e3-413a-bac6-13eea0063d14.

Chow, Clara. *Dream Storeys*. Ethos Books, 2016.

Comaroff, Joshua. "Built on Sand: Singapore and the New State of Risk." *Harvard Design Magazine*, No. 39 / Wet Matter, 2015.

Comaroff, Joshua, and Ong Ker-Shing. "Paramilitary Gardening: Landscape and Authoritarianism." https://whysingaporeblog.wordpress.com/wp-content/uploads/2016/09/paramilitary-gardening.pdf.

"Foreshores Act 1920." *Singapore Statutes Online*. https://sso.agc.gov.sg/Act/FA1920.

George, Cherian. *Freedom From The Press: Journalism and State Power in Singapore*. NUS Press, 2012.

Ghosh, Amitav. "Petrofiction: *The Trench* by Abdelrahman Munif." *New Republic*, March 2, 1992.

Gómez-Barris, Macarena. *The Extractive Zone: Social Ecologies and Decolonial Perspectives*. Duke University Press, 2017.

Husum, Hans, Swee Chai Ang and Eric Fosse, eds. *War Surgery, Field Manual, Second Revised Edition*. Third World Network, Trauma Care Foundation, 2011.

Jozuka, Emiko, et al. "Singapore Grand Prix: Humidity Meets Hedonism During Asia's Most Punishing Race." CNN Sports, September 25, 2019.

Knipe, Henry. "Progressive Supranuclear Palsy." *Radiopaedia.org*, May 7, 2025.

Ladurantaye, Steve. "A Potash Primer: What It Is and Where It Comes From." *Globe and Mail*, November 5, 2010.

Lauriston, Victor. "The Town of World Travelers." *Maclean's Magazine* 37, no. 9 (May 1924): 18–19, 65-66.

Lee, Kuan Yew. "Speech at a Convocation Dinner of the University of Singapore, Held at Adelphi Hotel on 19th June, 1967." National Archives of Singapore. www.nas.gov.sg/archivesonline/data/pdfdoc/lky19670619.pdf.

Lim, Charles. *SEA STATE*. www.seastate.sg/.

Lim, Irene. "Jurong Island." *Singapore Infopedia*, 2001. https://www.nlb.gov.sg/main/article-detail?cmsuuid=ad9dd6c3-782d-474c-a632-92d57ba9e1e3.

Loewenstein, Antony. *The Palestinian Laboratory: How Israel Exports the Technology of Occupation Around the World*. Verso, 2023.

Mam, Kalyanee. "Lost World." *Emergence Magazine*, Wilderness Issue, No. 2, 2018.

Ministry of Education (Singapore). "Supporting Our Students Through the Years—Evolution of Streaming in Secondary Schools." www.moe.gov.sg/microsites/psle-fsbb/assets/infographics/full-subject-based-banding/Evolution-of-Streaming.pdf.

National Parks Board. "*Samanea saman* (Jacq.) Merr." Flora & Fauna Web, last updated June 5, 2025. www.nparks.gov.sg/florafaunaweb/flora/3/1/3106.

Ng, Weng Hoong. *Singapore, the Energy Economy: From the First Refinery to the End of Cheap Oil, 1960–2010*. Routledge, 2012.

Riddle, Amy. "Petrofiction and Political Economy in the Age of Late Fossil Capital." *Mediations* 31, no. 2 (Spring 2018): 55–74.

Saskatchewan Government. "Saskatchewan to Build Partnerships in Singapore and Philippines." Press release, December 8, 2023.

Shreve, Ellwood. "$46M land claim vote delayed: Walpole Island may be entitled to much more, researchers say." *Chatham Daily News*, August 20, 2024.

Sim, Cheryl. "Little India Riot." National Library Board, February 16, 2015.

Singapore Graphic Archives. "Selling Weapons from Singapore." https://graphic.sg/collections/singapore-defence-industries.

Soh, Darren. *In the Still of the Night (While You Were Sleeping).* Self-published, 2015.

Soo, Jason (dir.). *1987: Untracing the Conspiracy: The Story of Operation Spectrum*. 2015.

Sorkhabi, Rasoul. "Miri 1910." *GeoExPro: Geoscience and Technology Explained* 7, no. 2 (2010).

ST Engineering. "Commemorative Books." www.stengg.com/en/about-us/our-history/.

Tan, Pin Pin, dir. *In Time to Come*. Singapore: BFG Media, 2017.

Tan, Pin Pin, dir. *To Singapore, With Love*. Singapore, 2014.

Tanzer, Andrew. "Houston of Asia. (Singapore)." *Forbes* 145, no. 11 (1990): 124.

Teo, You Yenn. *This Is What Inequality Looks Like*. Ethos Books, 2018.

Tomba, Mattia, ed. *Beating the Odds: 50 Years of Singapore-Israel Ties.* World Scientific Publishing, 2019.

Variety. "'Westworld' Creators Jonathan Nolan & Lisa Joy Preview Season Three." YouTube, March 14, 2020. https://youtu.be/t81OwGtwwyQ?si=aZaYBI-31qUpPeIl.

Walsh, Sean P. "The Roar of the Lion City: Ethnicity, Gender, and Culture in the Singapore Armed Forces." *Armed Forces & Society* 33, no. 2 (2007): 265-285.

Wee, Jason. *In Short, Future Now: on a post super future asia . . . a poem.* Sternberg Press, 2021.

Wenzel, Jennifer. "How to Read for Oil." *Resilience: A Journal of the Environmental Humanities* 1, no. 3 (Fall 2014): 156-161.

Wilkinson Eyre. "Competition Film, Gardens by the Bay, Singapore." YouTube, September 15, 2017. https://youtu.be/OcfSSyVWNYc?si=1whhZ9YGPtUhyHVc.

Wills, Eric. "'Westworld' and the Architecture of Dystopia." *Architecture Magazine*, April 28, 2020. www.architectmagazine.com/design/westworld-and-the-architecture-of-dystopia_o.

Wong, Pei Ting. "Jail for Man Behind Missing Bullet That Sparked 14-Day Search Involving Police, Army." *Todayonline*, December 28, 2018.

Zhao, Robert Renhui. *The Land Archive: Singapore 1925–2025.* Platform 2014. www.landarchive.org/main.html.